The Singularity of Literature

What is literature? What makes a text "literary" and how do we explain its extraordinary ability to unsettle, intoxicate and delight its readers? Throughout the centuries, influential thinkers have struggled with these questions, but no one has succeeded in pinning down the essence of literature. Derek Attridge invites us to take this resistance to definition as a starting point, in order to explore afresh not only literature, but the wider practices of Western art.

Drawing on a range of philosophical traditions, Attridge here crystallizes many years of thinking about what happens when a writer produces an innovative work or a reader responds to it, at the time of writing or much later. He brings out the implications of regarding the work as an event performed anew each time by the reader, responding to its singularity, inventiveness and otherness. Calling for a "responsible" form of reading that does justice to these aspects of the work, Attridge retheorizes the place of literature in the realm of the ethical. His theory is anchored in scrupulous practice through new readings of well-known texts and, for those wishing to trace the theoretical underpinnings of key arguments or explore the major issues in greater detail, an appendix of "debts and directions" is provided.

Returning to arguments begun in his influential volume *Peculiar Language*, Derek Attridge here provides us with a remarkable new framework for the discussion of literature and the literary. Never losing sight of the pleasures of the text, this book will inspire all those who teach, study or simply enjoy what we call "literature."

Derek Attridge is Professor of English at the University of York, UK, and Distinguished Visiting Professor at Rutgers University, USA. He is the author and editor of acclaimed volumes on literary theory, beat prosody, sixteenth-century poetry and twentieth-century fiction.

Also by Derek Attridge

As author

Well-weighed Syllables: Elizabethan Verse in Classical Metres

The Rhythms of English Poetry

Peculiar Language: Literature as Difference from the Renaissance to James Joyce

Poetic Rhythm: An Introduction

Joyce Effects: On Language, Theory, and History

Meter and Meaning (*with Thomas Carper*)

J. M. Coetzee and the Ethics of Reading: Literature in the Event

As editor

Post-structuralist Joyce: Essays from the French (*with Daniel Ferrer*)

Post-structuralism and the Question of History (*with Geoff Bennington and Robert Young*)

The Linguistics of Writing: Arguments between Language and Literature (*with Nigel Fabb, Alan Durant, and Colin MacCabe*)

The Cambridge Companion to James Joyce

Acts of Literature, by Jacques Derrida

Writing South Africa: Literature, Apartheid, and Democracy 1970–1995 (*with Rosemary Jolly*)

Semicolonial Joyce (*with Marjorie Howes*)

James Joyce's *Ulysses*: A Casebook

In praise of this book

"A wonderfully original and challenging book . . . *The Singularity of Literature* is written with remarkable clarity, succinctness and economy. I do not know of any other book quite like it."
J. Hillis Miller, UCI Distinguished Research Professor, University of California, Irvine

"Inventive, novel, singular, just. These words not only define the theory of literature propounded in this book, they also describe the virtues of Derek Attridge's writing. Circling around the claim that the singularity of literature is an irruption of otherness into the field of our experience, the event of an invention, Attridge builds a powerful account of literature and an original account of the relation of literature to ethics. Written accessibly and without jargon, this book will excite old and new readers of literature alike."
Simon Critchley, Professor of Philosophy, New School University, New York, and the University of Essex.

"This is an extraordinary book—richly original, timely and profound."
Henry Staten, University of Washington

"The best intellectual workout I have had in quite some time. It has a great many virtues, not least among them its very conciseness, its capacity to reward theory novices and veterans alike, and its timeliness in reassessing the nature and purpose of literary study at the cusp of the new century. There is, in short, nothing else like this book in terms of range, scale, accessibility, significance, and just plain smartness."
Andrew Parker, Amherst College

" A brilliant, major theoretical work that will change 'literary studies' as a term and as a discipline."
Kathleen Davis, Princeton University

"A truly important contribution to the study of literature and the arts."
Michael Eskin, Columbia University

The Singularity of Literature

Derek Attridge

Routledge
Taylor & Francis Group

LONDON AND NEW YORK

First published 2004
by Routledge
2 Park Square, Milton Park, Abingdon, Oxon, OX14 4RN

Simultaneously published in the USA and Canada
by Routledge
270 Madison Ave, New York NY 10016

Routledge is an imprint of the Taylor & Francis Group

Transferred to Digital Printing 2005

Typeset in Galliard by Keystroke, Jacaranda Lodge, Wolverhampton

British Library Cataloguing in Publication Data
A catalogue record for this book is available from the British Library

Library of Congress Cataloging in Publication Data
Attridge, Derek.
  The singularity of literature / Derek Attridge.
    p. cm.
Includes bibliographical references and index.
  1. Literature—Philosophy. I. Title.
  PN49.A75 2004
  801—dc22

                                    2003020809

ISBN 0–415–33592–2 (hbk)
ISBN 0–415–33593–0 (pbk)

For Suzanne

An absolute hospitality . . . graciously offered beyond debt and economy, offered to the other, a hospitality invented for the singularity of the new arrival, of the unexpected visitor.

Jacques Derrida, *Of Hospitality*, 83

To introduce a meaning into Being is to move from the Same to the Other, from *I* to the other person; it is to give a sign, to undo the structures of language. Without that, the world would know nothing but the meanings that inform the minutes or reports of corporate board meetings.

Emmanuel Levinas, writing on Blanchot, in *Proper Names*, 147

. . . the process called poetic invention that mingles breath and sense in a way that no one has explained and no one ever will.

Elizabeth Costello, in J. M. Coetzee, *Elizabeth Costello*, 98

Contents

Preface

What does it mean to respond to a work of literature as literature? When we read a novel, attend the performance of a play, or hear a poem on the radio, we are clearly doing many different things at once and experiencing many different kinds of pleasure (or displeasure). Which of these things is a response to specifically *literary* qualities? Can these qualities be found in works that are not normally classified as literature? And what kind of importance should we attach to them?

These are old questions, to which many answers have been suggested, and yet they remain puzzling. The new answers proposed in this book (some of which are old answers reinterpreted) arise from my own experience of literature, and art more generally, and from my engagement with philosophical discourses directly or indirectly concerned with such experiences. If I advocate the rethinking of a number of concepts familiar in the tradition of literary criticism – among them meaning, form, context, reading, inventiveness, responsiveness – this is because I believe that literature, fully appreciated, demands such a rethinking.

A great many others have responded in recent decades to these demands, and if *The Singularity of Literature* had been a different kind of book, it would have been awash with citations and references. However, my aim has been to write as accessible a work as possible, and I have therefore resisted the temptation to identify precursors and allies, engage in polemic, and situate my thinking in the various debates that have churned around the topic for a very long time. Instead, I have added a short appendix in which I try to be explicit about my major intellectual debts and to point out avenues for further reading.

I began trying to write about these questions with a double-barreled project in mind: a theoretical discussion of literature and the literary combined with a reading of J. M. Coetzee's fiction, an *oeuvre* which explores and exemplifies with particular intensity and urgency the theoretical issues I wanted to follow up. It eventually became clear to me that I would have to write two books, and the poetry-centeredness of the examples in this book will, I trust, be made up for by the detailed readings of prose fiction in *J. M. Coetzee and the Ethics of Reading*. I have allowed occasional references to Coetzee's writing to remain as indications of its importance in the book's genesis.

This book owes far too much to far too many people to allow proper acknowledgment here. In the appendix, I mention the many friends who have over a long period helped me understand the importance and implications of Derrida's work. More specifically, I have had valuable feedback on the manuscript from Kathleen Davis, Michael Eskin, J. Hillis Miller, Andrew Parker, and Henry Staten. Others with whom I have had instructive conversations about the topics broached in this book include Peter Edmonds, Tom Furniss, Marjorie Howes, Julian Patrick, Bruce Robbins, Mark Sanders, Peter Osborne, Meredith McGill, Elin Diamond, and Carolyn Williams. The last four were, like me, members of the Center for the Critical Analysis of Contemporary Culture at Rutgers University, New Brunswick, in 1997–8; for a year of immensely pleasurable learning I extend my thanks to all the seminar members as well as to the Director of the Center, George Levine. Students in my graduate classes at Rutgers were an abundant source of stimulation and reformulation, and I was led to many valuable clarifications and necessary complications by questions after talks on various aspects of this project at the Universities of Oxford, Sussex, Stockholm, Stirling, Salford, Essex, Waterloo, and Western Ontario, Amherst College, the State University of Arizona, Manchester Metropolitan University, New York University, and Queen's University, Ontario. I thank Lindsay Waters for suggesting an apt title. Liz Thompson at Routledge has been all one could wish for in an editor.

This book reworks arguments, and sometimes repeats phrasing, first published in two essays: "Innovation, Literature, Ethics: Relating to the Other" (*PMLA* 114 [1999]: 20–31) and "Singular Events: Literature, Invention, and Performance," in *The Question of Literature*, ed. Elizabeth Beaumont-Bissell (Manchester University Press, 2002, 48–65). Material from the first of these is reprinted by permission of the copyright owner, the Modern Language Association of America, and from the second by permission of Manchester University Press. Some paragraphs have been derived from another essay: "Literary Form and the Demands of Politics: Otherness in J. M. Coetzee's *Age of Iron*," in *Aesthetics and Ideology*, ed. George Levine (Rutgers University Press, 1994, 243–63, copyright © 1994 by Rutgers, The State University; reprinted by permission of Rutgers University Press). I am grateful to Jonathan Ball Publishers (Pty) Ltd for permission to reprint "The actual Dialogue," by Mongane Wally Serote, first published by Ad. Donker (Pty) Ltd in 1973 in *To Whom It May Concern*, edited by Robert Royston.

For financial and institutional support that allowed me time to read, think, travel, discuss, and write, I am glad to acknowledge the John Simon Guggenheim Memorial Foundation, the National Endowment for the Humanities, Rutgers University, the Camargo Foundation, and the Leverhulme Trust. My daughters Laura and Eva have constantly provided the most welcome of distractions, and my parents-in-law Ronald and Joyce Hall have been a sustaining and cheering presence. The debt I owe to Suzanne Hall goes far beyond anything I can express here or signal in dedicating this book to her.

York, 2003

Introductory 1

Opening questions

There is no shortage of testimony, in the pages of daily and weekly publications, in reading groups and book clubs, in off-the-cuff comments, to literature's unsettling, intoxicating, moving, delighting powers. A small number of philosophers and literary theorists have taken these powers seriously without, on the one hand, attempting to reduce them to a system or, on the other, taking refuge in vagueness and irrationalism. And there are some signs of an increasing willingness among those who study literature to address, as an issue of major importance, the question of aesthetic effect (as well as aesthetic affect), thus restarting a very old debate that had, for a time, almost fallen silent. I do not wish to begin, however, as many theoretical accounts of literature do, with the various philosophical projects that have largely determined our approach to these issues and the vocabulary we use, but rather with the observable phenomena themselves: the paradoxes inherent in the way we talk about literature, the pleasures and the potency that we experience in reading it.

My title, *The Singularity of Literature*, may be heard as an echo of that of an earlier book of mine, *Peculiar Language*. The arguments I work through in this book arise to some degree from the argument in that study: to put it over-simply, that all attempts since the Renaissance to determine the difference between "literary" and "non-literary" language have failed—and that this is a *necessary* failure, one by which literature as a cultural practice has been continuously constituted.[1] In pursuing further this question of literature's evasion of rules and definitions, and trying to elucidate my own experience of and pleasure in particular works of literature, I have found myself coming back again and again to two issues that have received much acknowledgment in passing but surprisingly little close attention as theoretical questions that extend well beyond the particular histories of artistic movements. The first of these is the role of *innovation* in the history of Western art;[2] the second is the importance to readers, viewers, and listeners of the *uniqueness* of the individual artwork and of the artist's *oeuvre*. I redefine these two widely acknowledged properties of art and of our understanding of art under the names "invention" and "singularity" (giving the book's title a second implication), and bring them into conjunction with another property that has been much discussed, though also much abused, in recent theoretical writing: "alterity" or "otherness." Such a coming-together involves more than a conjunction, in fact: I see invention as inseparable from singularity and alterity; and I see this trinity as lying at the heart of Western art as a practice and as an institution.[3] This conception of the artwork brings into focus two further dimensions which, I believe, are crucial to our understanding of it: its occurrence as a particular kind of *event* to which I give the name "performance," and its participation in the realm we call "the ethical." These topics are all addressed in the chapters that follow.

That the history of Western art in all its genres is a history of innovation—a long sequence of artists or groups of artists constantly searching for new modes of expression to exploit, new facets of human life to represent, new shades of feeling to capture—is a familiar fact, but the significance of this fact has not always been appreciated. That we can read a poem or watch a play written hundreds or even thousands of years ago and feel we are experiencing directly its creator's inventiveness is a phenomenon most of us would recognize, but accounts of this phenomenon have tended either toward the mystical or the dismissively demystifying. That we experience literary works less as objects than as events—and events that can be repeated over and over again and yet never seem exactly the same—is something many have acknowledged, but the implications of which few have pursued. In all our transactions with art, whether as creators, consumers, critics, or dealers, we put a premium on the uniqueness of the work and the distinctiveness of the *oeuvre* or school, yet our aesthetic theories often make little of this central fact. And although many attempts have been made to describe or analyze the act of creation, artistic or otherwise, few of these face head-on the puzzle which it entails: how does an entity or an idea unthinkable or unimaginable within existing frameworks of understanding and feeling come into being as part of our understood and felt world? And why is it so often described by creators not as an experience of doing something but of *letting something happen*?

This could have been a book about art in its widest sense, and I hope it will be read with profit by some whose particular interest is in an art-form other than literature. It is only by an artificial and often arbitrary act of separation that the qualities of the literary can be discussed, as I shall for the most part be doing, in isolation from related qualities in other art-forms. My decision to limit the discussion to literature springs from two sources: a hesitation to make pronouncements about other fields in which I have less training and experience, and the realization that the need to pay due attention to the specificity of each art-form would result in a book much longer and more unwieldy in its argumentative procedures than I was willing to contemplate. Although I give some attention to "the singularity of literature" in the sense of its difference from other art-forms, I do not discuss those other practices as such. However, there is some consideration of the aesthetic field more generally in the early chapters and an occasional glance toward other art-forms in the rest of the book. It would not, I believe, be an especially difficult task to extrapolate from the main points of my characterization of literature to the wider arena, including those developments in electronic media that may—who knows?—spell the end or at least the transformation of the verbal arts as we presently understand them.

Since my claim is that literature, or rather the experience of literary works, consistently exceeds the limits of rational accounting, what I offer is less a logical argument than a report and an invitation: a report on a certain living-through of the literary, and an invitation to the reader to share, at least for the duration of the reading, this living-through. In the interests of economy and pace, I limit literary examples to a few short poems; this may skew the argument to some degree, but not, I hope, damagingly. (In Chapter 8 I discuss the possible objection that my approach privileges poetry over other literary modes.) I refer the reader to my companion book, *J. M. Coetzee and the Ethics of Reading*, for further exemplification of these arguments.

One point that needs to be made clear is that this attempt to understand the "literariness" of certain written texts is not an attempt to state what is *most important* about such texts in our private lives and social existence. Importance can be measured in many ways, and in our day-to-day lives the scale on which the literary comes high may not be a scale that counts for a great deal. We rightly value the works belonging to the tradition of literature for a number of different things they are capable of being and doing, most of them not strictly literary. Poems such as Henley's "Invictus" or Kipling's "If" have clearly given comfort or courage to thousands, but it is not obvious that it is as literature—in the sense which I try to develop in this book—that they possess this remarkable and much prized power. A work like the *Iliad* or *Beowulf* can serve as a rich source of historical information; Fielding's and James's novels may be instructive in the art of moral living; Zola and Stowe perhaps played a part in ameliorating the lives of many individuals in unhappy circumstances: none of these capacities, however, falls peculiarly within the literary preserve. My argument is that literature, understood in its difference from other kinds of writing (and other kinds of reading), solves no problems and saves no souls; nevertheless, as will become clear, I do insist that it is *effective*, even if its effects are not predictable enough to serve a political or moral program.

Understanding "literature"

Do the terms "literature," "the literary," and "literariness" refer to actual entities—objects, institutions, or practices—to be found in certain cultures at certain times, or are they categories that have come into being as a way of organizing and simplifying the complex and fluid processes of linguistic production and reception in those cultures? Where such questions are taken seriously today, the second of these alternatives is no doubt the favored one, and for good reason: there seem few grounds for thinking that the concepts named by these terms correspond in a one-to-one fashion with objects or patterns of behavior that exist independently of the language that labels them. There have been many discussions of the long and convoluted history of the idea of literature, and of the closely related (though significantly different) histories of similar concepts named in other Western languages, which serve as valuable reminders of the complicated past and continuing ambiguity of this group of interrelated words.

But in order to understand the importance today of this cluster of terms and concepts to the broader web of ideas and practices that make up what we call Western civilization, and thereby perhaps to encourage fresh thinking about the future direction of that civilization, it is necessary to embark on something other than cultural history or lexicographical investigation. Literature always seems to present itself in the final analysis as something *more* than the category or entity it is claimed to be (writing that has a particular institutional function, say, or writing with a particular relation to truth), and as valuable for something *other* than the various personal or social benefits that are ascribed to it. This "something more" or "something other" remains obscure, however, although many different attempts have been made to specify it.[4] It is as if the linguistic and intellectual resources of our culture, while registering the importance of the property or process or principle to which the term "literature" and its cognates serve as witnesses or which they bring into being, are unable to provide direct access to it.

Analytical language is already beginning to break down in my attempt at lucid exposition. I have employed the words "property," "process," and "principle" to refer to what it is that literature might be said to witness or bring into being in the full knowledge that all these words are unsatisfactory, as, in this sentence, is the use of the word "it" and the notions of "witnessing" or "bringing into being." This difficulty is, of course, a direct outcome of the curious state of affairs we are discussing: were it possible to find unambiguous names, to use pronouns with confidence, to talk in terms of simple acts of referring or constituting, there would be no need to ascribe to the non-discursive mode of literature a peculiar potency not possessed by other linguistic practices. There is something fundamentally paradoxical, perhaps even wrong-headed, in an attempt such as the present one to use a non-literary discourse to convey what literature, most importantly, can do. Nevertheless, there might be some profit in pursuing the attempt to the extent that theoretical and descriptive language will allow it, as a corrective to other—often even more reductive—accounts of literature, and as a complement to the primary activity of the reading of the works we call literary.

Although I have acknowledged that the entities named by the terms under scrutiny—the (ill-defined) body of literature, individual literary works, the practice of reading those works, and the literary as a property of certain texts—can be thought of as in fact produced by the concepts that appear to designate them, it is also the case that the difficulties that beset any theoretical analysis derive from the resistance of those categories to the process of conceptualization. If the term "literature" does not uncomplicatedly name something in the world, it does not uncomplicatedly bring something into existence either. Rather, by putting the processes of naming and constituting themselves into play, by, in a sense to be developed later, *performing* them, it complicates that very opposition. Literature may be a cultural product, but it is never simply contained by a culture.

Literary instrumentalism

> Once a professor of modern languages, he has been, since Classics and Modern Languages were closed down as part of the great rationalization, adjunct professor of communications. Like all rationalized personnel, he is allowed to offer one special-field course a year, irrespective of enrolment, because that is good for morale. This year he is offering a course on the Romantic poets. For the rest he teaches Communications 101, "Communication Skills," and Communications 201, "Advanced Communication Skills."[5]

J. M. Coetzee's satiric portrayal, in his 1999 novel *Disgrace*, of the impact of reductive, management-driven methods on universities, and on their teaching of literature in particular, no doubt struck many a chord among its readers in a number of countries. The plethora of fashionable buzz-words that emerged in the world of education during the last two decades of the twentieth century—quality assurance, benchmarking, accountability, outcomes assessment, performance indicators, and all the rest of them—are symptoms of an attitude toward teaching and learning, and toward what we can loosely call the aesthetic domain, that is far from new—Dickens parodied it in *Hard Times*, Weber, Adorno, and Horkheimer in their very different ways addressed it as a significant historical phenomenon—but that is now, as one aspect of increasing globalization, permeating more areas and activities than ever before.

A large majority of literary critics, scholars, theorists, and historians have been strongly opposed to this approach as it has manifested itself in the policies of government departments, funding bodies, and educational institutions. It is regarded, quite rightly, as a threat to much that is valuable in humanistic learning. However, some of the modes of literary study that became popular in the same period might be said to share to a certain degree its underlying assumptions, or at least to operate with a notion of literature that poses no challenge to those assumptions. Let me, for the sake of brevity though at the risk of oversimplification, give it the single label "instrumentalism," collapsing together under this term a diverse but interconnected group of preconceptions and tendencies.

What I have in mind could be crudely summarized as the treating of a text (or other cultural artifact) as a means to a predetermined end: coming to the object with the hope or the assumption that it can be instrumental in furthering an existing project, and responding to it in such a way as to test, or even produce, that usefulness. The project in question may be political, moral, historical, biographical, psychological, cognitive, or linguistic. This book is an attempt to conceive of literature (and by implication other artistic products and practices) in a different light, as, in fact, defined by its *resistance* to such thinking. In doing so, I have been able to draw on a number of thinkers who have made similar attempts—most important to me in this regard have been Derrida, Blanchot, and Adorno—but whose arguments have not had the impact on our practices of literary commentary they deserve.

What I am calling an instrumental attitude to literature, I must at once add, is a necessary one for most of our dealings with verbal texts: it enables us to process them efficiently, it prevents the continual re-evaluation of our beliefs and assumptions, and it is in accord with the main function of most of the writing and speech we encounter. In the field of literary studies, this attitude has been highly productive, giving us valuable accounts of literary works as indices to the historical, sociological, and ideological texture of earlier periods and other cultures and to the psychic and sometimes somatic constitution of authors, injecting literature into political struggles (in the name of humanism, the working class, oppressed races and nationalities, women, and homosexuals, to name just a few), and exemplifying in literary works important features of linguistic structure, rhetorical and formal organization, and generic conventions. The experience of immediacy and vividness which we often gain from literary works of the past leads naturally to their being pressed into service as a source of evidence for lives led before ours or in foreign places; and although there is a danger that the "reality effect," the created illusion of a real referent, may interfere with as much as it aids accurate historical and human judgment, the judicious use of literary evidence is clearly as valid as other modes of access to a vanished or otherwise inaccessible culture.

Literature's powerful effects, and the high estimation it is accorded in cultural formations, inevitably lead also to its being appealed to and utilized when a political or ethical cause is being fought for. Although there is an inescapable tendency on the part of those whose professional lives center on literature to exaggerate its potency as a political weapon, there is no doubt that it has had a role to play in significant, and frequently laudable, social changes, like the ending of slavery or the reduction in the use of capital punishment in some parts of the globe. Its complex handling of language makes it a prime source, too, of linguistic and stylistic investigation and education, even though its complexity is sometimes too great for a science that is still finding extraordinary complications in the operation of simple sentences. In all these ways, literature functions, and is made to function, as a powerful and invaluable instrument of individual and social advancement.

There is a quite different sense in which an instrumental attitude operates as a motive force in the academic study of literature. The desire to be noticed, to gain promotion and material rewards—a desire which it would be foolish to try to condemn or proscribe—continually produces new readings of literary works and new goals for reading,[6] Graduate students frequently choose courses or dissertation topics, with eminent good sense, on the basis of their usefulness for their chosen career, rather than on the intellectual provocations and rewards they might offer; articles and books are written with an eye to the market-place and the syllabus; and "theoretical approaches" are mastered (or their salient catchphrases learned) in order to utilize them efficiently in reading and writing instead of being approached with an openness that allows for a range of possible outcomes—including a challenge to the very project they are supposed to be serving. Instrumentalism of a kind is evident every time a commentator observes, disparagingly, that such-and-such a theoretical approach or literary preference is now "out of date," as if their value resided wholly in their fashionableness and marketability.

No doubt it has always been thus in human dealings with language; even when some kind of space has been made for a non-utilitarian linguistic or semiotic practice, it has quickly been transformed by the pressures of survival and competition into a tool. But it is evident that instrumentalism has become unusually dominant in the academy in recent years, as it has in all spheres of education, and it is now something of a rarity to encounter a response to a literary or philosophical work which attempts to postpone the moment of purposive co-option, or a theory which argues for the importance of such an attempt. It would be naïve to think that reading could be innocent of exterior motivations and goals, if only because since Marx, Darwin, and Freud we know how little we can be aware of the hidden processes and drives that condition our plans and performances. There is, however, an obvious distinction between a reading that sees as its task the pragmatic utilization of the work it reads and one that comes armed (or rather disarmed) with a readiness to respond to the work's distinctive utterance and is prepared to accept the consequences of doing so.

This shift to an increasingly instrumental approach to literature is, of course, part of a more general, globally experienced increase in the weight given to the values of the market-place, to the success ethic, to productivity as a measure of worth. Everything I have said about attitudes to works could be said about attitudes to other persons and other cultures. Although the majority of recent studies claiming a political function for literature to have appeared in recent years have situated themselves on the left, there is a sense in which many of them could be said to participate in an instrumentalized system of literary education, criticism, and publication. Bitterly opposed though Margaret Thatcher and Ronald Reagan were by the majority of literary academics, their governments' profit- and productivity-oriented approaches came to pervade the academy—not so much by dint of persuasiveness or example, but by the creation of a situation of reduced resources and increased competition and an ethos founded on self-promotion and material accumulation. Their successors (of whatever political party) have done nothing to reverse this shift.

The instrumental approach that dominates literary criticism today has produced a number of extremely original and illuminating works;[7] and the fact that it has also produced a number of pedestrian or incoherent works—works, for instance, based on a crude notion of the relation between "text" and "context," or on a wild overestimate of the power of literary works to effect political change—is largely a function of the inevitable unevenness in quality of the works that spring from any fertile cultural movement. One often hears the claim that there has been an overall decline in the quality of published literary criticism (using the word to cover all kinds of commentary and editorial scholarship), but this is a highly problematic, and inescapably ideological, assertion— as well as one which was never, and probably never will be, *not* made. However, the second type of instrumentality I have mentioned—the increasingly powerful operation of the market-place in the academy, the success which follows from success—could well explain any recent increase in the proportion of under-researched and self-advertising books. The role of "theory" in any such account is a complex and interesting one: in the 1970s and 1980s it provided exactly the influx of new terminology and approaches needed to build successful careers on, even though, taken seriously, much of the work being so utilized presents a strong challenge to instrumentalism of this kind.

The success—in both the intrinsic and the market sense—of the worthwhile and important studies in this instrumental mode has had another effect (not necessarily an intended one, and admittedly one which has operated in concert with a number of other forces): the diminishing of careful attention to the specificity of the literary within the textual domain, and to the uniqueness of each literary object. Most extended complaints about this change have come from commentators who are nostalgic for a time "before theory"—a time, that is, when the governing theoretical and ideological assumptions of literary study went largely unacknowledged and unexamined—and who yearn for a "simpler" critical style based on a love of literature and of individual works. This nostalgia and yearning are not simply to be dismissed: as an understandable reaction, they are a significant reflection of the state of affairs I am delineating, and my aim in this book is to find a more cogently articulated framework within which to account for, and perhaps rearticulate, these feelings and needs.

Some varieties of cultural studies include an overt argument against making *any* distinction between literary and other works, and this is an argument that has to be taken seriously—indeed, it is one that I wish to grant almost in its entirety. That "almost," however, is the subject of this book.

The aesthetic tradition

To raise the issue of the specificity of literature and the uniqueness of the literary work is to raise the issue of *form*, or at least those aspects of textual production which have traditionally gone under that name. (Of all the many ways in which the authors of the entry under "literary" in the *Oxford English Dictionary* might have defined the term in its modern sense, the one they plump for is the following: "Pertaining to, or having the characteristics of that kind of written composition which has value on account of its qualities of form.") It is difficult to imagine a characterization of literature as a distinct linguistic domain that would not in some way or other invoke its formal features, although there is little agreement as to exactly what these are. The only exception is an understanding of literature which assumes that it is totally determined by the choices of those who put it to the particular use (or find in it the particular uselessness) which the theory in question associates with the literary; and even in this scenario it is likely that the works chosen by the culture as "literary," though they may not be intrinsically different from other works, are viewed through a lens which heightens attention to their formal properties.

Similarly, the question of the specificity of the individual literary work is inevitably tied up with the question of its form. The writer's sense that a work is finished, that after a process of repeated revision it seems "right" (at least for the moment), and the reader's sense of an integrity, a quiddity, a singular and strong identity, stem from the shaping of language and not from some set of ideas or emotions which the work encodes. (Works that flout formal integrity and closure are effective only because of the expectations they thwart.) Of course, the notion of "form" has a lengthy and troubled history, and at the beginning of the twenty-first century it is not possible to make a straightforward appeal to any such notion to solve our problems about the distinctiveness and value of the literary. In Chapter 8 I reconsider the role of formal features in our experience of the literary work and the relation of form to meaning and context, approaching these questions by a route rather different from the one traditionally followed.

In turning to issues of form as an antidote to an overemphasis on instrumental approaches to literature, we inevitably find ourselves confronting the long and rich tradition of aesthetics. This, at least, is the shorthand name that tends to be used to refer to the vast and various body of debate about the experience and importance of the artistic work in terms of some version of the "beautiful," existing in a sphere separate from the practical or utilitarian and governed by purely, or largely, formal considerations. (The tradition of aesthetics can be approached from other angles, of course, such as the emphasis given in early uses of the word to the operation of the senses—an emphasis ultimately derived from Plato, and not one with which I am directly concerned here.[8]) Although the most significant origin of this tradition is no doubt the philosophy of Kant (in spite of the fact that Kant's major emphasis was on natural, not artistic, beauty), its most influential recent exemplification in literary studies in the English-speaking world was New Criticism. In fact, the use of the past tense is inaccurate, since New Critical preconceptions and procedures—born in the second third of the twentieth century—still govern a great deal of literary pedagogy and critical practice, as a glance at most "introductions to literature" will quickly reveal.[9]

One undoubted reason for the recent flourishing of instrumental approaches in literary studies is the perceived inadequacy of the account of literature provided by the aesthetic tradition as mediated by New Criticism and similar critical approaches. It is not just that this tradition has failed to provide for any means whereby literature might intervene beneficially (or at all) in the political realm; more importantly, it has often been shown that assertions, explicit or implicit, of universal and permanent qualities in art-objects can be traced to an ideological interest operating within a specific historical situation. It is the recurrent self-contradiction visible within aesthetic commentary as it grounds transcendental arguments on unadmitted contingent factors that renders it unsatisfactory: all its discussions of artworks necessarily stop short of total explication (which would remove the defining quality of artistic activity, its inaccessibility to mechanical rules) and gesture instead toward a domain of ineffable, unknowable, transcendent principles that turn out on inspection to look a lot like the governing, and class-determined, canons of taste, or some identifiable reaction against these.[10]

The aesthetic tradition thus unwittingly demonstrates the powerful social determinants of the artwork and its reception; but to say this is not necessarily to dismiss as valueless its insistence on the impossibility of reducing the artwork to rules. Such an insistence seems to reflect a valid insight into the peculiar nature of art as a practice and institution characteristic of Western cultures. The institution of literature, for example, seems to be defined by its capacity to outstrip any precise specifications or predictions of what constitutes a "good" literary work; if the rules that have hitherto governed the production of such a work were to be fully specified, making possible a computer-driven assembly line turning out good novels, plays, and poems, these products would immediately fail to satisfy the demands of readers who value literature. The result of this situation would be either new works defying these rules, or an end to literature in anything like its present form. This is not to say that such an exhaustive explanation is inherently impossible —that would imply a mystical understanding of the literary which is not mine—but to insist that innovation and unpredictability have been central to the practice and appreciation of Western art from its beginnings to the present day. The implications of this fact have seldom been pursued with the attention they deserve.

Beyond aesthetics?

What is needed, therefore, to complement the instrumentalist achievements of recent criticism and to build on the lasting, if partial, insights of the aesthetic tradition is a mode of attention to the specificity and singularity of literary writing as it manifests itself through the deployment of form (a term which will require redefinition), as well as to the unpredictability of literary accomplishment that seems connected with that deployment—an approach that at the same time fully acknowledges the problematic status of all claims to universality, self-presence, and historical transcendence. This would not, I hasten to add, be a mode of criticism that had no connection with questions of politics or ethics (this would hardly be possible), or that portrayed literature as without value or effects in the world; my quarrel with what I am terming instrumentalism is that it judges the literary work according to a pre-existing scheme of values, on a utilitarian model that reflects a primary interest somewhere other than in literature. If literature rests on a certain inaccessibility to rules, as the aesthetic tradition recognizes, there is no way it can serve as an instrument without at the same time challenging the basis of instrumentality itself. Furthermore, a responsible textual instrumentality can rest only on readings that are themselves responsible, and there is currently a great danger that the works being invoked as keys to historical understanding or political progress will not be attended to with sufficient scrupulousness to allow them to complete (which will usually also be to complicate) the task they are called on to perform.

What about those old companions of the literary, truth and beauty? I am not arguing that literature has nothing to do with truth, though I have inherited a slight queasiness about the word that inhibits an entirely unqualified use of it. My thinking about this question is undoubtedly influenced by what has been called "post-aesthetic" theorizing about art, a response to the increasing dominance in Western culture over the past two centuries of an idea of truth that relies on the exclusion of normative and aesthetic values, an idea that has been central to the rise of scientific disciplines and achievements.[11] This conception of truth—as the production of statements which correspond to facts and which enunciate permanent and universal laws about those facts (a conception which has recently begun to be questioned within some scientific disciplines themselves)—gave birth to, and depended upon, a conception of the aesthetic as having, by contrast, nothing to do with truth. In the twentieth century, a number of thinkers—among them Heidegger, Adorno, and Derrida—have attempted to understand artworks in ways that challenge this separation between the domain of the aesthetic and the search for truth. The result of this challenge is that literature *can* once more be seen as participating in the telling of truths, but "truth" is no longer to be understood in the terms which once enabled it to appear as the privileged preserve of science, of the non- or even anti-aesthetic.

The experience of beauty, so crucial to the aesthetic tradition and so clearly an important aspect of our response to many works of art, cannot be taken as a defining property, both because its extension to all art is problematic and because it is equally an aspect of our response to many natural objects. Indeed, if the project of determining what is distinctive about literature, or art more generally, is to have any success, it must overcome the tendency to blur the boundary between the artifactual and the natural produced by an emphasis on beauty. The pleasures we take in works of literature are many, and enjoyment of beauty is doubtless often one of them, but let me emphasize once more that my aim in this book is not to offer a description of *everything* that can matter in the literary field, but to home in on what makes literature a singular phenomenon among all our experiences of language.

No doubt there will always be a degree of special pleading in the production of an account of a valued cultural practice when the writer shares the culture's valuation, as, by and large, I would say I do: I am (probably more than I realize) motivated by a desire to justify my own considerable expenditure of time and effort on literature, my determination to instill in others a sense of its worth, and my feeling that the pleasures it offers are more substantial than many others I experience, or can imagine experiencing. No doubt, too, such an argument will be received more enthusiastically by those who share this valuation of the literary than by those who do not. However, these are reasons for care and caution in constructing an argument, not for abandoning the project. The discussion of creativity that follows has a direct bearing here: a discursive text which does nothing more than produce justifications for an existing preference by means of commonly accepted arguments may win widespread approbation but is much more likely to be subject to the deformations of special pleading or, in the psychoanalytic sense, rationalization, than one which takes risks in an attempt to break down existing habits of thought and open itself to possibilities of innovation. Whether this book does so is not, of course, for me to say.

In approaching the issue of literature's distinctiveness, I begin obliquely, with one of the most salient and vexing questions of our time: What is entailed in responding to otherness? Or, to put it differently, I begin where I am, now, here, writing these words, trying to do justice to thoughts I have not yet been able to formulate.

Creation and the other   2

Creating

I sit at my desk with my computer monitor before me and my keyboard beneath my hands, writing. What exactly am I doing as my fingers press the keys and my eyes scan the screen? One answer would be that I am attempting to express my ideas in words. If that is the case, I must already know in some fashion what those ideas are, and the activity I am engaged in is a form of translation, a trying-out of different words until I hit upon the ones that match the idea I want to express. Leaving aside the problems raised by the notion of a pre-verbal idea, it may be that what I am engaged in for much of the time that I am writing is not far from this kind of translation. In this case, when I have formed a sentence to my satisfaction the feeling I have is that it encapsulates something I wanted to articulate without at first having the appropriate words, or, more accurately perhaps, without my words possessing the required linear and organized sequence.

However, there are times when this description will not do, when I am not putting into words a conceptual structure I have already planned, not tinkering with an existing text to make it more accurately express what I know I want to say, not working out a problem according to a pre-existing set of rules, but engaging in an activity we may call, to give it one of its possible names, "creation."[1] It is a common enough activity, with analogues in many other fields, but one that resists precise terminology and has seldom been scrutinized—perhaps because it *is* so familiar. I seem to be composing new sentences out of nothing, or rather out of a largely inchoate swirl of half-formulated thoughts and faint intimations; from time to time the nebulous outlines take shape as phrases or argumentative links, but I keep losing the thread, deleting, going back over my typed words, making one more attempt to say what needs to be said, or even, it sometimes seems, *demands* to be said. What I have to resist is my mind's inclination toward repetition, its tendency to process any novelty it encounters in terms of the familiar. Motivated by some obscure drive, I sense that I am pushing at the limits of what I have hitherto been able to think.[2]

It is extremely difficult to talk about the activity of linguistic (or any other) creation, which usually remains mysterious to the creator— indeed, some degree of inexplicability is often taken to be definitive of creation, in contrast to the simple act of production in accordance with existing models and rules. Although I began this chapter with an attempt at introspection, I am not seeking a psychological description or explanation of the process of creation (which would be the answer to a different question from the one I am asking), but rather an account of what exactly it is that is brought about by the psychological mechanisms employed—which may differ immensely from person to person and occasion to occasion. As I shall have reason to reiterate at several points in this book, what I am trying to shed light on is not at bottom a matter of psychology, consciousness, or subjective experience, but of structural relations, or, better, shifts between different structural relations and the possibilities and constraints they bring into being— which might include a revaluation of such concepts as the "psyche," "consciousness," or "experience."[3]

Most of the time, of course, there is a direct psychological correlate of creative activity. This psychological correlate provides much of the evidence for any examination of the creative process, but it is not the heart of my concern. The fact that much of the vocabulary available to us has psychological connotations, however, means that my focus may seem to be on the mental and emotional events involved in writing and reading, and it is important to note that the question I am asking is not "What psychological processes are involved in the act of writing and reading creatively?" but rather "What does it *mean* to say that a particular act of writing or reading is creative?" My interest is in a structural, sequential relation between two states, the nonexistence and the existence within a culture of a particular kind of entity. (One of Coetzee's characters reflects with wonder on Shakespeare's creation of a particular phrase: "Out of the dark emerging, out of nowhere: first not there, then there, like a newborn child, heart working, brain working, all the processes of that intricate electrochemical labyrinth working. A miracle."[4]) Although the question of the mental activities involved in this transition from non-being to being is a fascinating one and constantly borders on the questions we are asking, it has recourse to different kinds of evidence and looks for different kinds of answers. Since Kant and Schelling (and in England, Blake and Coleridge), a central term in accounts of creation in the sphere of art, and sometimes in other spheres as well, has been "imagination": this is an example of a term that places the psychological activity of the individual at the heart of the creative process, and is therefore only of limited use in the present discussion. Our question is: how does it happen that, via the work of an individual or a group of individuals, otherness enters, and changes, a cultural sphere? This is not a question which is simply about the activities of a psychological subject.

Although I have been using, and will continue to use, the word "experience" a great deal, this should not be understood as inevitably implying conscious experience: in the discussion that follows, to experience something is to encounter or undergo it, to be exposed to and transformed by it, without necessarily registering it—or all of it—as an emotional, physical, or intellectual event. (It will be clear at once that what I am articulating is very different from the traditional concept of "aesthetic experience.") As I have noted, the "experience" of alterity may challenge and refashion the concept of experience itself.

How, then, can we describe verbal creation? (The reason for asking this question is not just its inherent interest: an understanding of what creation means will shed light in due course on the process of reading and responding to literary works.) One approach that will allow us to develop a fuller account is to say that it is a handling of language whereby something we might call "otherness," or "alterity," or "the other," is made, or allowed, to impact upon the existing configurations of an individual's mental world—which is to say, upon a particular cultural field as it is embodied in a single subjectivity.[5] Otherness is that which is, at a given moment, outside the horizon provided by the culture for thinking, understanding, imagining, feeling, perceiving.[6] (We shall have to complicate this notion of the "outside," and the implication of a simple opposition to the "inside," in due course; for the moment, let us just note that there is an important sense in which otherness is not simply "out there" but is produced by the same operations that constitute what is familiar.) An alternative term for otherness might be "newness," but this term—although I shall use it from time to time—has the disadvantage of suggesting a historical narrative whereby the old is constantly displaced by the new, whereas in fact it is often through the old that otherness makes itself felt.

Otherness is not something the would-be creator can simply take hold of, as an idea, a formal possibility, a mathematical equation, lying outside familiar frameworks. The creative mind can work only with the materials to which it has access, and it can have no certain knowledge beyond these; it therefore has to operate without being sure of where it is going, probing the limits of the culture's givens, taking advantage of their contradictions and tensions, seeking hints of the exclusions on which they depend for their existence, exploring the effects upon them of encounters with the products and practices of other cultures. Accounts of creative activity, in a number of fields, regularly use terms like "trial and error," "hunch," "guess," and "lucky break." The very term "experiment" paradoxically combines the notions of a controlled, repeatable physical process and the unpredictable trying-out of new procedures.

To pause for a moment on an example, we may say that in order to be able to write *Pride and Prejudice*, Jane Austen must have had a profound awareness of the resources of the English language, the conventions of the novel, the stylistic palette of humorous writing, and the norms of individual morality and social interaction, as these all existed in late eighteenth-century British metropolitan culture, and the ability to draw on them to produce fiction of extraordinary richness and subtlety. At the same time, the only way to explain the novel's leap into new territory is to say that in the process of manipulating these familiar materials (in her head and on paper) she must have been drawn—perhaps without realizing it was happening—to exploit their discontinuities, press at their limits, and extend their capacities, and that in so doing she found a work of startling newness emerging. Both these descriptions must be true, not in the sense of psychological and biographical accuracy, but as accounts of the shift from the non-existence of *Pride and Prejudice* to its existence. (In fact, what emerged in 1796–7 was a novel she called "First Impressions," and one indication of its unprecedentedness was its rejection by the publisher to whom she submitted it.) The creative writer registers, whether consciously or unconsciously, both the possibilities offered by the accepted forms and materials of the time, and their impossibilities, the exclusions and prohibitions that have sustained but also limited them. Out of the former emerge reworkings of existing models, out of the latter emerges the otherness which makes these reworkings new works of literature.

Culture and idioculture

My account of creation, like much of this book, makes free use of the term "culture," but this does not mean I believe it to be an unproblematic term; far from it. "Culture" has a huge range of meanings, a diversity which can make for imprecision and inconsistency. However, in this discussion its large scope brings some advantages, as I need a term that includes, among other things, the artistic, scientific, moral, religious, economic, and political practices, institutions, norms, and beliefs that characterize a particular place and time. (*How* particular a place and time—whether one means what we rather too easily call "the West," a single self-defined "people," a nation-state, or a city, and whether one means a century or a decade—depends on the context of the argument. Other determinations have to be factored in as well, such as gender and class.) I am not using the term to make a sharp distinction between the "cultural" and the "natural"; on the contrary, I take the relation between the human and the non-human in all its forms to be a significant part of what I am calling "culture."

My particular interest is in the way an individual's grasp on the world is mediated by a changing array of interlocking, overlapping, and often contradictory cultural systems absorbed in the course of his or her previous experience, a complex matrix of habits, cognitive models, representations, beliefs, expectations, prejudices, and preferences that operate intellectually, emotionally, and physically to produce a sense of at least relative continuity, coherence, and significance out of the manifold events of human living. I shall use the term "idioculture" to refer to this embodiment in a single individual of widespread cultural norms and modes of behavior. Although a large part of an individual's idioculture may remain stable for some length of time, the complex as a whole is necessarily unstable and subject to constant change; and although one is likely to share much of one's idioculture with other groups (one's neighbors, one's family, one's age peers, those of the same gender, race, class, and so on), it is always a unique configuration. The fullest verbal representations of idiocultures are probably to be found in fictional works: Joyce's *Ulysses*, for instance, is an exploration of the idiocultures of two Dublin men (and for the space of one long chapter, a Dublin woman) on a particular day in 1904. Even this highly detailed accumulation of memories, habits, associations, inclinations, fears, doubts, hopes, and desires as they manifest themselves in the space of a few hours is nothing but a fraction of what makes up an individual idioculture.

The complexity of a cultural field or an idioculture is something we can barely fathom; it is certainly not something to which we can achieve direct access. Although we may speak of a culturally defined group's encounter with otherness, the actual encounter is always, of course, that undergone by individuals within the group, and thus differs from person to person and moment to moment. We should not, however, think of idioculture in primarily psychological terms, even though it has psychological manifestations; the purpose of introducing the term is to be able to talk about the subject as a node within a set of noncontinuous and heterogeneous networks. Idioculture is the name for the totality of the cultural codes constituting a subject, at a given time, as an overdetermined, self-contradictory system that manifests itself materially in a host of ways. At the same time, it is important to note that individuality is not *exhausted* by idioculture; that is to say, I am more than the sum of the parts of cultural systems I have absorbed. I am not only unique, in the sense that no one else is constituted by exactly the same idioculture; I am—and this distinction will become clearer in later chapters—singular.[7]

The creation of the other

The phrase I have used for the title of this section, "the creation of the other," can be read in two ways.[8] If it is taken to be derived from "creating the other," it emphasizes agency and activity: to be truly creative is to wrest from the realm of the familiar the hitherto unthought, to bring into existence by skillful and imaginative intellectual labor an entity that is irreducibly different from what is already in being. Such an account does not seem entirely true to the process I am trying to describe, however. In a curious way, the ideas I have not yet been able to formulate seem to be "out there" rather than simply nonexistent, although I know this is not literally the case. My experience has an element of passivity, of attempting to heighten responsiveness to hints of relationships, to incipient arguments, to images swimming on the edges of consciousness, an element of "letting them come" as much as seeking them out.

When I write a sentence that seems "just right" although I could not have predicted it, a sentence that pleases me with its encapsulation of a point I had not known I was about to make, I am not able to say how it came into being, but I *can* say that I did not produce it solely by means of an active shaping of existing, conscious, mental materials.[9] Although we need to exercise caution in deducing structural processes from psychological experiences, it seems likely that this passivity is an important aspect of the coming into being of the new. If this is true for minor achievements of creative articulation such as the account of literature I am engaged in, it seems likely that major feats of creativity spring from a much more remarkable openness of the mind to what it has not yet grasped.

Hence the appropriateness of the alternative reading of the genitive construction in "the creation of the other," according to which my text, and perhaps something of myself, are created *by* the other. Countless writers have testified to this experience; here is Coetzee's characteristically perspicuous account:

> As you write—I am speaking of any kind of writing—you have a feel of whether you are getting closer to "it" or not. . . . It is naïve to think that writing is a simple two-stage process: first you decide what you want to say, then you say it. On the contrary, as all of us know, you write because you do not know what you want to say. Writing reveals to you what you wanted to say in the first place. In fact, it sometimes constructs what you want or wanted to say. What it reveals (or asserts) may be quite different from what you thought (or half-thought) you wanted to say in the first place. That is the sense in which one can say that writing writes us. Writing shows or creates (and we are not always sure we can tell one from the other) what our desire was, a moment ago. (*Doubling the Point*, 18)

Philosophers often make similar remarks about their breakthroughs; this is Derrida: "I am hovering around a hypothesis, a logic, an analysis, and suddenly a word appears as the right one to exploit, thanks to its formalizing economy. . . . The feeling I have is not of having invented or of having been the active author of this thing, but of receiving it as a stroke of luck."[10] Even the comedian experiences something of this sort: Mike Nichols is reported as saying, "When a joke comes to you, it feels like it's been sent by God."[11]

This alternative meaning for "the creation of the other" should not be taken to imply a mystical belief in an exterior agent; rather, it indicates that the relation of the created work to conscious acts of creation is not entirely one of effect to cause. The coming into being of the wholly new requires some relinquishment of intellectual control, and "the other" is one possible name for that to which control is ceded, whether it is conceived of as "outside" or "inside" the subject. (What happens, in fact, is that the simple opposition of inside and outside is broken down, as is the sense of an integrated and active subjectivity.) Furthermore, if the settled patterns of my mental world, the norms of my idioculture, have been so freed up that the truly other finds a welcome, my subjectivity will have been altered in some degree, and thus—especially if the cumulative effect of such events is taken into account—the self too can be said to be a "creation of the other." In fact, as I shall argue more fully below, when I encounter alterity, I encounter not the other as such (how could I?) but the remolding of the self that brings the other into being as, necessarily, no longer entirely other.

The value of a single phrase which invokes both these perspectives on the coming into existence of the new is that it fuses what might otherwise seem different processes or opposing accounts.[12] It thus achieves what a logical or discursive account could not—the phrase is itself, in other words, an example of a creative use of language. It is thus a minor exemplification of the demands made by our subject-matter on the mode of argument: in attempting to specify what the singularity of literature consists in, we cannot proceed wholly in accordance with the norms of logical reasoning or philosophical discussion. What the phrase highlights is that novelty is achieved by means *both* of the refashioning of the old *and* of the unanticipated advent of the new; or, more accurately if more paradoxically, that the advent of the new *is* a particular kind of refashioning of the old. We may say that the other's arrival destabilizes the field of the same, or that the destabilization of the field of the same occasions the arrival of the other; both these statements are true, though each is incomplete without its counterpart. Most of the time, our accounts of this process have to veer between narratives that suggest the energetic reshaping of existing configurations in order to produce the new—forging it in the smithy of one's soul, for instance—and narratives that suggest the passive experience of the other's irruption into the settled order—the most common of which has been inspiration by the Muse or some other external and inscrutable power.[13] Thinking creatively about creation means thinking of these as two sides of the same coin.

In order to do this, we need to return to the question of cultural richness, and the complexity of the idioculture by means of which an individual participates in his or her cultural contexts. At any given moment, this complexity is a divided and contradictory one, its semblance of coherence sustained by the repression or exclusion of some elements and possibilities, subject to constant challenge from the outside as well as to ongoing tensions within. (Could we examine it diachronically, we would find that its unstable complexity is the product of a history of irruptions of alterity, partly assimilated, partly resisted.) I am always, in a way, other to myself. It is this instability and inconsistency, these internal and external pressures and blind spots, this self-dividedness, that constitute the conditions for the emergence of the other (which can be a hitherto unperceived relationship, a different way of handling materials, a new method of production—the list is endless).[14] The other brought into being in a creative event is thus at once implicit in the cultural field and wholly unpredictable from it.

This is why creation is as much a matter of alertness to hints of as yet unexplored possibilities as it is of skillful handling of known materials. By contrast with creation, straightforward *production*, what is often called "making," introduces no alterity and instigates no transformation of the cultural field: it redeploys existing components according to accepted norms. The existence of this contrast should not be taken to suggest, however, that these are two entirely separable ways of working with cultural materials; the point at which making becomes creating, or creating reverts to making, is never predictable, and can be assigned only after the fact.

Nor need creation be dramatically sudden. It is often a gradual process of false starts and wasted efforts, erasures and revisions, slowly inching nearer to an outcome that, one can only hope, will be the desired one, or arriving at it in fits and starts. We may quote from Coetzee's *Disgrace* again, though this description of David Lurie's composition of a chamber opera is the echo of thousands of similar accounts across a number of fields:

> And, astonishingly, in dribs and drabs, the music comes. Sometimes the contour of a phrase occurs to him before he has a hint of what the words themselves will be; sometimes the words call forth the cadence; sometimes the shade of a melody, having hovered for days on the edge of hearing, unfolds and blessedly reveals itself. As the action begins to unwind, furthermore, it calls up of its own accord modulations and transitions that he feels in his blood even when he has not the musical resources to realize them. (183–4)

There is always an element of risk in the process of creation, of trusting to the future, of a certain helplessness in the face of what is coming. Failure is frequent, when the otherness that seemed to be on the horizon turns out to be another version of the same; conversely, success can often look like failure at first. Nor is creation usually a matter of choosing a problem to address or a goal to achieve and then getting down to work: though this may be the way the process starts, the initial problem or goal is very often displaced in a wholly unexpected outcome.[15]

Creation, then, is both an act and an event, both something that is done intentionally by an effort of the will and something that happens without warning to a passive, though alert, consciousness. Since there is no recipe, no program, for creation, it cannot be purely a willed act. (This is not the place to discuss the possibility that creation is, in part at least, an "act" of the unconscious: my argument could certainly be recast in psychoanalytic terms, although this would raise a number of different questions.) However, since creation requires preparation and labor, it cannot be purely an event.[16] Moreover, each of these aspects of creation can be described in two ways: the act of breaking down the familiar is also the act of welcoming the other; the event of the familiar breaking down is also the event of the irruption of the other. (I use the verbal phrase "break down" because—another creative possibility of our language—it can refer either to an act or to an event.[17]) If one is able to break down the old in a creative and not just a negative manner (and at the time it is not possible to be sure which of these one is doing), the new comes into being; at the same time, the breakdown of the old is produced by the pressure of its internal contradictions—which, since its contradictions are a function of what it excludes, is the same as saying that it breaks down under the pressure of the other.

Since the other is manifested only in a dynamic process, there would be some justification for jettisoning the noun in favor of a verb; even the terms "event" and "eventness" are misleadingly nominal, abstracting away from the happening they name. Otherness exists only in the registering of that which resists my usual modes of understanding, and that moment of registering alterity is a moment in which I simultaneously acknowledge my failure to comprehend and find my procedures of comprehension beginning to change.

Accommodating the other

Imagine a philosopher struggling with a problem over a long period, then experiencing a mental breakthrough that makes it possible for her to resolve the once impenetrable difficulty. It is likely that from then on she will be able to go through the arguments without trouble, what was other having been wholly accommodated, and the changes in mental organization that made this possible having become permanent.[18] To take a different kind of example, an inventor labors for months trying to make a better mousetrap and finally succeeds, thanks to an idea that comes to him one day from out of the blue: he is unlikely to find himself ever again baffled by the problem he had set himself (and he may become a millionaire). In this process, the shifts in the subject's frameworks of understanding and feeling which make possible the acknowledgment—which is at the same time the advent—of the other in an event of creation produce a lasting change in idioculture; the other may be said to become the same, but that "same" is not the same as it was before the encounter.

On the other hand, if I write a few paragraphs that surprise, please, and move me with their images and formulations, their otherness may survive to challenge my habitual processes of thought and feeling on many future occasions. Although I sense the rightness of what I have accomplished, I do not wholly understand what this consists in, how it produces its remarkable effects. Each time I read what I have written, I undergo (though never in quite the same way) an encounter with alterity, which is to say the shifting and opening-up of settled modes of thinking and feeling. In such a case, the idiocultural displacements which made the creative event possible have not produced a permanent transformation; alternatives just glimpsed as the other became the same have receded again as old habits have reasserted themselves, only to flicker up again on re-reading. In this case what I have to offer the world is the possibility not of a new structure of knowledge but of a powerful and repeatable *event* of mental and emotional restructuring. Whatever formula may be deduced (by others or by myself) from my work as the basis for further works does not exhaust or fully explain what I have achieved. I have created, that is to say, a *work of art*—or, to be more precise, a potential work of art. (We will turn to the question of reception in later chapters.)

To create an artwork, then, is to bring into existence a configuration of cultural materials that, at least to a certain group and for a certain time, holds out the possibility of a repeated encounter with alterity. In the case of most types of invention, once it has brought about change in an individual or a culture its work is done: its effects will continue to be felt through those applications, reproductions, and reworkings. The artistic invention is strikingly different: though it too gives rise to repetitions and developments of various kinds, it retains its inventiveness as long as it finds a responsive audience, which is to say as long as it is not wholly and permanently accommodated.

The distinction I am drawing here between accommodation and non-accommodation should not be thought of as absolute. For one thing, resistance to accommodation can occur only in the context of the process of accommodation, and may be felt merely as a coloring of or hesitation in that process. Moreover, the instability and mutability of idiocultural norms mean both that accommodation can never be permanently assured, and that a hitherto unaccommodated other may always make itself wholly at home. And when we come to look at the way in which a created work can spawn further events of creation, we shall find a further reason to complicate this account.

Versions of "the other"

"The other," it must be granted, is a somewhat overworked phrase in current academic discourse, and may seem too portentous or too imprecise for my purposes here, but it has certain merits. One is its implication that, although the kind of encounter I am discussing happens repeatedly and to everybody, it is always a *singular* encounter, and an encounter with singularity. Alternatives such as "otherness" and "alterity" are rendered somewhat less useful by their generality, their suggestion that we are dealing with a substance that could be spread about or divided up.[19] The otherness that is brought into being by an act of inventive writing—an argument, a particular sequence of words, an imagined series of events embodied in a work—is not just a matter of perceptible difference. It implies a wholly new existent that cannot be apprehended by the old modes of understanding, and could not have been predicted by means of them; its singularity, even if it is produced by nothing more than a slight recasting of the familiar and thus of the general, is irreducible.[20] "The new," while it has some advantages as a term, lacks—even with the definite article—this implication of singularity.

Another virtue of the phrase "the other"—in this case one it shares with "the new"—is that it is premised on a *relation*. To be "other" is necessarily to be "other than" or "other to." Many of those who use the phrase fail to acknowledge its relational implication, an error which is the source of many problems.[21] What is "the same" to me or to my culture is other to someone else or to someone else's culture, and vice versa. Moreover, it is other only in the set of circumstances within which a particular encounter takes place. There is no "absolute other" (or "Other") if this means a wholly transcendent other, unrelated to any empirical particularity—or if there is, it is a matter for religious faith alone.[22] It will already be evident that this complicates the account of singularity which I have just given. If the other is always and only other *to me* (and hence to my culture, as embodied in my idioculture), I am already in some kind of relation to it, and for two entities to exist in relation to one another is to share some general framework, however minimal. (My own singularity, too, is thus not a walled-in uniqueness.) Otherness, that is, is produced in an *active* or *event-like* relation—we might prefer to call it a *relating*: the other as "other to" is always, and constitutively, in the process of turning from the unknown into the known, from the other into the same. As important as the individual's new creation are the mental and emotional transformations that had to occur to make its existence (as singular-turning-into-general) possible. An entity without even this relation would simply not impinge on me; as far as I was concerned, it would be nonexistent.

The turn from the singular to the general that I am describing is not to be identified with such phrases as "the violence of representation" or "the domestication of the other." That model presupposes a narrative in which the other starts by being wholly different and is then stripped of its otherness so that it can be integrated or manipulated. In the account I am giving, the other is not this at first utterly inaccessible and then all too accessible entity. *Only in relating to me* is the other other, and its otherness is registered in the adjustments I have to make in order to acknowledge it—adjustments that may never become wholly second nature to me.

The other, therefore, does not have a prior and independent being which happens to be masked from me; it (which should probably be written "it," to indicate the inappropriateness of the pronoun one is forced to use) does not come from outer space but arises from the possibilities and impossibilities inherent in the culture as embodied in a subject or a group of subjects. (These possibilities and impossibilities arise, as we have seen, from the fact that the culture, like any idioculture within it, is not whole, stable, or homogeneous, that it depends on certain exclusions and marginalizations.) We are not talking about what is "ineffable" or "inexpressible" in a general sense, only what cannot be thought or said in a particular culture at a particular time. Absolute alterity, as long as it remains absolute, cannot be apprehended at all; there is, effectively, no such thing.

We can specify the relation between the same and the other a little more fully by thinking of it in terms of that which the existing cultural order has to occlude in order to maintain its capacities and configurations, its value-systems and hierarchies of importance; that which it cannot afford to acknowledge if it is to continue without change. These exclusions vary from the large-scale to the minute, from the ethically momentous to the ethically inconsequential. A particular way of thinking and feeling can mean that entire races are treated as lacking fully human status (the concept of "race" itself being one of the ways a culture effects such exclusions), or, to take an even wider category that is currently under pressure (and this includes pressure from inventive artists), that non-human animals are excluded from many ethical and political considerations. The transformations wrought when the racial other ceases to be other as a result of cultural change are wide-ranging—they include shifts in cognitive categories, in habits, in affective responses, in ethical judgments, and much else—and if a similar process is about to take place in regard to animals, even greater shifts may lie ahead.

To take an example at the other extreme, with no direct ethical or political implications, the formal subtlety and power of eighteenth-century English poetry depended on the non-acceptance of a number of possible metrical arrangements—which is to say that to the poetic mind of the period they were impossible. When these arrangements became possible, under the pressure of popular poetry and song, a new valorization of freedom, a less deferential attitude toward classical literature, and a number of other forces, the whole poetic landscape changed. A poem like Coleridge's "Christabel" at once exposes the limits on which earlier poets depended (in a highly fruitful way) and opens new avenues for future poets. Unlike the example of racial prejudice, this example from the realm of art shows that here we are not dealing with a necessary progression from worse to better: if value is to be accorded to the welcoming of the other, it has to be in terms of the benefits of change itself.

In discussing the relation of the other to the same, we face another terminological dilemma. Words such as "exclusion" and "margin-alization," although they are difficult to avoid, are misleading. They imply a knowledge of what lies beyond the limits, as well as a conscious decision to keep it there, whereas, as I have stressed, the other is that which is not knowable until by a creative act it is brought into the field of the same. An overt policy of racist exclusion or oppression does not raise the question of alterity; but we might use the word in talking about an ingrained racist ideology which makes it impossible for individuals to think in certain ways about other individuals. In the sphere of art, there is a second reason why "exclusion" and "marginalization" are inappropriate. They have a negative ring to them, whereas the limits that exist at any point in time are always enabling at the same time as they are restricting. (Racial, ethnic, or religious limits are also enabling, of course, but what they enable—a disparity of economic privilege and power, for instance—is morally unacceptable.) It is this combination of the simultaneous opening and closing of possibilities with each cultural shift that produces continuing instability, and thus continuing opportunity for change.

The encountered other

In many discussions from Hegel to the present, "the other" (or "the Other") possesses a somewhat different significance from the one I have selected. In particular, it indicates an already existing entity which the self encounters; most obviously, another human being. "The other" in Levinas's writing, for example—frequently called "*Autrui*" rather than "*l'Autre*" in order to bring out its human dimension—is linked closely to the biblical "neighbor," even though ultimately the otherness in question is that of God. In colonial and postcolonial studies "the other" tends to stand for the colonized culture or people as viewed by the dominant power.[23] Whatever its precise complexion, the other in these accounts is primarily an impingement from outside that challenges assumptions, habits, and values, and that demands a response.

How substantial is the difference between the other as an existing entity—such as a human being—to which I am enjoined to respond and the other as that which beckons or commands from the fringes of my mental sphere as I engage in a creative act? At first sight, they may seem to have little in common. In the former case, it might be said, the other is other because its substance, its center of consciousness, its ethical claim upon me, or some such fact about it is wholly beyond my grasp, wholly foreign to me and to my experience. In the latter case, the other is other only in so far as it has not yet come into being, as long as existing modes of thought or language, whose complexities, containments, and overdeterminations are its breeding ground, are incapable of bringing it to birth. When it *does* come into being it necessarily ceases, at least temporarily, to be other. In the first case we can pronounce the other as other, it seems, from the beginning of the encounter with it; in the second case it is only retrospectively and in the past tense that we can make this pronouncement, since during the process of creation all is risk, guess, potential, with no sure outcome, and after it the other has been accommodated by the same (albeit a different same). Our task in the first instance is to respond to the other as other, in the second to bring the other into being as something other than the other.

Yet this stark contrast does not survive closer inspection. For to the extent that I apprehend the "already existing other" in the form of a person it is not other: I recognize the familiar contours of a human being, which is to say I assimilate him or her to my existing schemata of understanding. One aspect of my response, it is true, may be an acknowledgment of the other person's subjectivity as impenetrable to mine, or an acceptance that his or her claims as an ethical subject are not limitable by mine. But these are responses to the person not as singular individual but as (generic) person, with an "equivalent center of self" to my own, "another origin of the world."[24] However, if in this process I remain aware, or become aware through an act of attention, of some failure in the process of assimilation, some strain or internal conflict in my categorization, I may be responding to the singular otherness of the other person. It is in the acknowledgment of the other person's uniqueness, and therefore of the impossibility of finding general rules or schemata to account fully for him or her, that one can be said to encounter the other as other—in the same moment that those rules and schemata shift, however momentarily, to take account of the now no longer other. While affirming the other as other, therefore, I encounter the limits of my own powers to think and to judge, my capacities as a rational agent. In this way, the encounter with a human other is not different in its essentials from the experience of the other as one attempts creatively to formulate fresh arguments or to produce an original work of art or philosophy.[25]

The response which seems to be called for by this glimpsed apprehension of otherness as a result of the failure of existing modes of thought and evaluation is therefore a kind of creation. To respond fully to the singular otherness of the other person (and thus render that otherness apprehensible) is creatively to refashion the existing norms whereby we understand persons as a category, and in that refashioning— necessarily inaugural and singular—to find a way of responding to his or her singularity. Moreover, respect for the singularity of the other person requires that *each time* we encounter him or her we do so with a readiness to be creative in our response—an imperative that also springs from the fact that he or she is no longer exactly the same person as before. "The other" in this situation is therefore not, strictly speaking, a *person* as conventionally understood in ethics or psychology; it is once again a relation—or a relating—between me, as the same, and that which, in its uniqueness, is heterogeneous to me and interrupts my sameness. If I succeed in responding adequately to the otherness and singularity of the other, it is the other *in its relating to me*—always in a specific time and place—to which I am responding, in creatively changing myself and perhaps a little of the world as well.

This process of responding to the other person through openness to change is not dissimilar, then, to the one that occurs when a writer refashions norms of thought to realize a new possibility in a poem or an argument. As has often been remarked, the sense the writer has when this happens is that of achieving what one was seeking (finding the appropriate word in a poetic line; articulating the next stage of an argument) and would be accurately expressed not by "At last, I have made something new!" but rather by "At last I have got it right!" or even "At last I have got it!"[26] Granted, it is presumably part of the writer's general intention to compose sentences that are different from anything written before, and that at the same time are intelligible, informative, pleasure-giving. But what is foremost in the creative mind is neither the issue of innovation nor that of communication; it is the demand being made for a just and generous response to thoughts that have not yet even been formulated as thoughts, feelings that as yet have no objective correlative. In responding to the other person, to the other as a person, a similar demand for justice is at work, requiring a similar step into the unknown. When we turn later in this book to the question of literary reading, we shall once more register the importance of the parallel between creativity and responsiveness, and the ethical significance of the attempt to do justice to the other in both.

Originality and invention 3

The concept of originality

Creation is a private event. It happens when an individual brings into being something hitherto beyond the reach of his or her knowledge, assumptions, capacities, and habits. When what is brought into being is also other to the norms and routines of the wider culture, our usual word for the quality thus displayed is "originality."[1]

To be creative is to make something new out of whatever materials one possesses; thus we have no difficulty in calling children creative, as they find new ways of deploying the limited cultural ingredients they have imbibed (even if what they create has already been created by a million other children). To be original, however, is to create something that marks a significant departure from the norms of the cultural matrix within which it is produced and received, a much rarer achievement. (That cultural matrix can be narrow or wide, but it does have limits; while it makes sense to say that Donne's lyrics are original in the context not just of English literature but also of European literature, it does not make sense to say that they are original in the context of world literature.) Just as creativity may not result in originality, so originality is not inevitably a sign of creativity: it is possible to be original by accident. However, the kind of originality that is central to our discussion is that which arises from creativity, and the kind of creativity we are interested in (I have already mentioned Jane Austen's as an example) is that which results in the coming into existence of original works.

It will be obvious that by "originality" we do not mean *any* difference between a given work and its predecessors in a certain field. Originality that is highly valued—as distinct from mere novelty—entails a particular kind of difference from what has gone before, one that changes the field in question for later practitioners. (This is as true for the sciences as for the arts.) The first thinker to articulate this distinction was Kant,[2] whose important contribution was to make a clear distinction between originality as mere difference—"nonsense too can be original," he observed—and what he termed "exemplary originality," a type of originality that, as a product of genius, provides both a pattern for methodical reproduction by future artists lacking in genius but adept at absorbing new trends and, more significantly, a spur to future geniuses for the further exercise of exemplary originality.[3] Artists of the former kind, by deducing the rules according to which the original work operates, only "imitate" it; those of the latter kind "follow" it by finding fresh ways to be original in response to its originality. From now on, I shall use "originality" only in the sense of exemplary originality.

The creative act, however internal it might seem, works with materials absorbed from a culture or a *mélange* of cultures, and it is upon cultures that it has its effects, if it has any. To be creative, in the limited sense in which I am using the term, the mind needs only the materials it happens to have, whether shared or not, but originality—which is the only way in which creativity can be culturally registered—requires a close engagement with the circumambient cultural matrix. The most innovative artists or scientists have usually had an exceptionally great capacity to incorporate cultural materials, and have therefore been able in turn to make the strongest impact upon their cultures. Nor is this merely a question of the richness and range of the stuff which the mind has to work on; what the original creator finds in the cultural field, as I have already suggested, is not just material but gaps in the material, strains and tensions that suggest the pressure of the other, of the hitherto unthinkable, of that which is necessarily excluded.

After the creation and reception of an original work, the cultural field is different; some old possibilities have disappeared and some new ones have been born—the latter consisting, as we noted earlier, both of formulae that can be imitated and of an unaccommodated alterity that may act as a spur to further originality. This explains why the history of Western art evinces very few retrograde movements, in which original work A creates the possibilities out of which original work B grows, and then work C is originated without taking any account of B, emerging instead out of the earlier changes instituted by A. Much more common is the sequence A—B—C, in which any reference C makes to A is colored by the changes in cultural conditions introduced by B.

Of course, it is not unusual for artists to be inspired by works of the past (we shall investigate this process in due course), and there have been frequent returns to earlier periods as strategies for the achievement of originality—to take one example, the Pre-Raphaelites' very name indicates the self-conscious deployment of this maneuver. These turnings-back, however, emanate from the conditions of their time as much as any other strategy of innovation. Artists who ignore the changed terms brought into being by their predecessors, however admirably their work may exploit the previously existing possibilities, create in a historical dead-end. Though we may enjoy their skillful manipulation of an earlier mode—think of the twentieth-century Gothic cathedrals in Liverpool and New York, for instance—we do not experience the exhilaration of new doors opening, fresh possibilities for creation emerging. Such works have, of course, no successors in a strict sense; to follow them is to follow the works they were modeled on, and only in their moments of originality (which both my examples certainly possess) can they provide a basis for further innovation.

Originality has sometimes been treated as though it were a defining feature of modern art—Pound's "Make it new!"—or as a brainchild of the Romantic period—Wordsworth's "great and original writer" who must "create the taste by which he is to be relished"—but it has unquestionably been (though not always under that name) at the heart of Western artistic practice and reception at least since Archaic Greek sculptors ceased to carve stiff-limbed *kouroi* under the pressure of a new manner of representing the human figure in stone, and probably since well before that.[4] It is true that the impulse to be creative has had a higher value attached to it in some eras than in others, and true, too, that if one is looking from a period such as ours in which originality commands a peculiarly high premium there is a tendency to overestimate its historical importance. Sometimes, too, familiarity makes it very difficult to take the measure of innovation in its own time.

This being said, however, it does not take much examination of the history of successive styles and generic norms in any Western art-form to realize that there has always been a drive to discover new formal arrangements, new relationships between art and the perceived world, new ways of exploiting the materials at hand in the world for what we now call aesthetic purposes. Histories of art, of music, of literature, almost always take innovation as their basic narrative principle. They often put names and dates to moments of breakthrough: Abbot Suger using pointed arches for his cathedral church at St Denis; Walt Whitman writing English verse without regular meter; Albrecht Altdorfer painting landscapes lacking in human figures or narrative; Buddy Bolden improvising trumpet solos in New Orleans—the list of such moments is extremely long, and would grow longer if we possessed more historical knowledge (a circumstance which would no doubt also serve to demolish many of our cherished examples). This is not to claim that innovation has always been undertaken and valued for the same reasons, or that it has always met with the same reception; what is undeniable, however, is that there is a striking continuity across thousands of years that, although it has been acknowledged in every history of art, has seldom been subjected to theoretical scrutiny.

It is not adequate to discuss this history of perpetual innovation under the rather dismissive rubric of "fashion," which is generally used to imply that the motor of change is an innate human tendency to boredom combined with a thirst for novelty, or, somewhat more analytically, a market economy requiring that consumers constantly be persuaded of the need to replace old goods with new, "improved" ones. While one must acknowledge that these factors do operate—under various guises—in the history of art, the nature of the changes and their effect on the cultural field suggest that there is more at stake; that innovation, although it is always unpredictable, can often be seen with hindsight to have arisen out of the specific conditions of the cultural field of the time and its relation to other fields such as the social, the political, and the economic. (This does not mean that it was the only possible development out of those conditions, even though in retrospect it may have the look of iron logic.) Existing artistic practices can come under pressure from a number of external sources, including those we might label technological (such as the ability to glaze larger spaces or use thinner materials), economic (such as the need to make do with diminished resources in times of hardship), political (such as the need for disguised expression in an occupied country), international (such as the impact of another culture after conquest or immigration), and ideological (such as the inadequacy of traditional artistic models in a post-revolutionary situation). These external pressures often serve to make visible rifts and stresses in what had been taken for granted as a fulfilling and self-sufficient mode of artistic expression, as when the couplet came, toward the end of the eighteenth century, to seem a restrictive and over-intellectual manner of writing poetry, or the vast scale of human misery came, toward the end of the following century, to seem under-represented in fiction.

The formal conventions of a given art-form at a given time thus both provide the ingredients for the creation of artworks and set limits on that activity, and changing demands and expectations often shift the balance from possibility to limitation.[5] Although the cultural matrix at a given time occludes what I am calling "the other" by allowing only a small proportion of the theoretically possible array of intellectual and artistic formations to occur, it also provides, in its internal differences and external conflicts, the conditions for the irruption of the other, via the creative labor of the artist. The music of Schoenberg could not have immediately followed the music of Bach, since Bach does not make Schoenberg possible; Wagner, however, does. This does not mean that the only way music could go after Wagner was toward atonality; to claim this would be to deny the unpredictability of art and the alterity of the artwork. Nor does it mean that art "progresses" or "develops" from inferior to ever more superior modes: although at any given historical moment, some modes of creation will be more responsive to the demands of the time (and the beckoning future) than others, there is no guarantee that they will preserve their advantage. The future will present new demands no less exigent and complex than the old ones, and the unremitting drive toward originality in relation to whatever cultural framework is prevailing at the time pays no heed to any larger narrative of "progress" or "improvement."

What the Russian Formalists called "defamiliarization"—the use of literary devices to render unfamiliar that which through habit has become scarcely noticeable—plays a part in this process of continuous innovation, but it is far from the whole story, and the Formalists' faith that what shines through by virtue of these devices is "reality" cannot be justified. The other is not the real, but rather a truth, a value, a feeling, a way of doing things, or some complex combination of these, that has been historically occluded and whose emergence or re-emergence is important for a particular time and place. (We shall return later to the question of the kind of importance this emergence may have.) Originality in the fullest sense is achieved when a combination of external and internal pressures makes it possible for a gifted individual or group to create a work of art that, as we say, breaks new ground, or, in the terms I have been using, brings about the irruption of the other into the same.

Experiencing originality

While we may be said to *appreciate* the originality of, say, James Watt's or Marie Curie's work, we are less likely to be said to *experience* it. Sometimes, however, we may directly encounter the evidence of highly original endeavors in the scientific and mechanical field, and find that the latter term is appropriate. To examine one of John Harrison's surviving chronometers is to experience a keen sense of the creativity that made precise navigation at sea possible; and the more familiar one is with the historical significance of his achievement, the stronger that sense becomes. I have no doubt that someone conversant with the history of mathematical thought may undergo a similar experience in reading or re-reading parts of Newton's *Principia Mathematica* or Tarski's *Logic, Semantics, and Metamathematics*.

In the field of art, this kind of experience is much commoner. To attune oneself to the elaborate delicacy of thirteenth-century Italian painting and then come upon Giotto's frescoes in the Arena Chapel is to be stunned not merely by the vividness and directness of the portrayal of human emotions but also by the gap these images suddenly open up between themselves and the earlier artistic mode that we have internalized: we feel the excitement of discovery, of a technical advance that is at the same time a shift in the possibilities open to visual representation. To listen to a series of symphonies by Haydn and Mozart and then to the opening bars of Beethoven's *Eroica* is not only to be swept into a rhythmic and harmonic world of immense suggestiveness but also to register, with unmistakable pleasure, the extraordinary achievement of bringing such music into being at a particular point in the history of symphonic style.[6] In experiences of this kind, we are clearly responding to what I am calling the originality of the work of art. We can, of course, make mistakes about this—taking a work to be much earlier or later than it in fact is, or failing to realize that it is only an imitation of a genuinely path-breaking creation—and these mistakes can affect our appreciation and judgment when we acknowledge them. To many viewers Van Meegeren's imitations of Vermeer seemed powerfully original works until it turned out that they were not by the master, a discovery which immediately converted the paintings to programmed applications of stylistic principles.

This experience of originality in the past is, it goes without saying, dependent upon familiarity with the background against which the new work appeared. To encounter fully the exhilarating newness of Dante's *Divine Comedy* we would need to steep ourselves in Italian, and particularly Florentine, cultural history of the late thirteenth and early fourteenth centuries; to read widely and intensively Dante's predecessors and contemporaries; and to come as close as we can to replicating in our own minds the habits, assumptions, and expectations of the place and period that saw the emergence of Dante's poem. Although such an enterprise could of necessity succeed only to a very limited degree—and there would be no way of knowing how far it had succeeded—there is no doubt that it would have a significant effect on our appreciation and enjoyment of Dante's work. In fact, most of us, when we read the writers of the past, rely on the insights of scholars who have set themselves something like this task, insights which filter their way into introductions, notes, lessons, films, and the hundred different channels whereby our understanding of literary works is enriched by information beyond what we glean from the text itself. The closer we are to the work's cultural envelope, its time, its place, its class and generational situation, of course, the more directly its originality, or lack of it, feeds into our response.

Clearly, the experience of originality can be a powerful and plea-surable element in our present enjoyment of a poem, a painting, a string quartet, even though it is an attribute located in the work's past. But we have not succeeded in accounting for the intensity and directness of the effect many works have upon us, often without our possessing any knowledge of their place in the history of art. We need to turn to other aspects of innovation to account for this crucial dimension of artistic engagement.

Inventiveness and invention

In spheres other than art, the terms "original" and "originality" are more or less synonymous with the terms "inventive" and "inventiveness." One difference between them, however, is that the latter pair suggest more strongly the activity of mind needed to create an original entity or idea, that is, an *invention*. And an advantage of the word "invention" for our purposes is that, like "creation," the same term is used for both an event and its result—so that our name for the object brought into being, when perceived as an invention, does not entirely divorce it from the process of its making.[7] An invention in the commonest sense may be a new device, program, or technology, but the act (which is also, as we have seen, an event) of invention is a mental feat, a step into the unknown, which makes possible both the manufacture of the new entity and, perhaps even more importantly, new instances of inventiveness in the culture at large.

Invention can be directly contrasted with creation, therefore, in a way that originality cannot, and we may pause a moment on this contrast as it applies both to art and to other fields, before turning our attention to the peculiarities of the former.[8] Creation is the bringing into being of something new to the creator, and is fully realized in the object (whether mental or physical) that is created. When the event of creation is *also* an event of invention, however, its effects go well beyond the created entity. An invention possesses originality of the fullest kind, Kant's exemplary originality; it is a new deployment of materials that can be both imitated and inventively developed, parodied, challenged.[9] If an invented entity—a philosophical argument, a scientific theory, a political institution, a work of art—is wholly accommodated by the culture, it may through this accommodation bring about permanent alterations in cultural norms, permitting others to employ the new configuration freely but uncreatively (perhaps without being aware of its origin). On the other hand, the process of apparent accommodation—the emergence of new norms and principles—will often destabilize the cultural field afresh, since those new formations will themselves depend on exclusions and exert pressures. In this case, we can say that accommodation is only partial; and it is out of such partial accommodation that further invention—always an engagement with the potential alterity implicit in the system—arises.

The old meaning of "invent," as "to find" (as in the rhetorical process termed *inventio*), is not irrelevant here: the testimony of countless artists, writers, scientists, and others—which should be taken seriously and not, as so often, dismissed as naïve or mystifying—shows that the experience of invention is an experience of coming upon a form, a phrase, a solution that seemed, in retrospect, to have been waiting in advance, or even one of being *found by* the form, phrase, or solution in a moment of illumination. Once again, Derrida's double-headed phrase is pertinent: invention is always the invention of the other. And the other does not exist as an entity, but is lived through as an event. (I do not wish to make a sharp distinction between "invention" and "discovery" in the field of scientific knowledge: the invention of a mechanical device may involve the discovery of a physical principle, while the discovery of a cure may require just as much inventiveness as the creation of a new type of engine.)

There are, of course, a number of pragmatic issues at work in determining whether a private creation achieves the status of a public invention. A created entity that has the power to bring about significant changes may be ignored for a number of reasons. Its influence may be diverted, diminished, overshadowed by the circumstances of its production or by contemporaneous events elsewhere. History has no reputation for fairness in this regard. An inventive event may be registered, or, more precisely, may occur for the first time, after a lag of several years or even several generations. Eugen Slutsky's revolutionary essay on consumer economics went unnoticed from its publication in 1915 until the mid-1930s; Gregor Mendel's inventive elaboration of the laws of heredity in the 1860s had to wait half a century before it had its full effects upon the science of biology and the practices of agriculture. Hence inventiveness is not an inherent property of an act or a created object; it can only be retrospectively, and never permanently, assigned. If one wished to talk about some feature of the object itself, one could refer to its "potential inventiveness"—but this is not a property that could be measured, since there is no place outside the varied events of reception where one could stand in order to do the measuring. Inventiveness is not, however, simply a property conferred by an external and arbitrary history: an invention always engages closely with cultural practices and systems as it deforms or disjoins them, and so the inventive act must already have a more-than-casual relation to the contingencies that surround it and that will influence its fate.[10]

What is an invention in the eyes of its creator, therefore, actually becomes one only in its reception by the culture at large. Otherness, as I have stressed, is a strictly relative term—otherness is always otherness to an existing subjectivity or state of affairs—and this is why the inventor has to be exceptionally well attuned to his or her cultural surroundings. Many a work that in the view of the scientist, artist, or philosopher who created it brings something new into the world turns out, when received widely, to be the familiar in superficially different dress.

Invention in art

We have seen that the originality in its own time of a work of art, of engineering, of mathematics, or of philosophy can be registered and enjoyed at a later time in an exercise of historical imagination. A curious and important feature of the innovative quality of many past works of art, however, is that they may produce a sense of newness and freshness, of bringing otherness into being, *in the present*. A typical articulation of the experience I am referring to is F. R. Leavis's, commenting in 1936 on the *Oxford Book of Seventeenth Century Verse*:

> After ninety pages of (with some minor representation) Fulk Greville, Chapman, and Drayton . . . we come to this:
>
> > I wonder by my troth, what thou, and I
> > Did, till we lov'd? were we not wean'd till then?
> > But suck'd on country pleasures, childishly?
> > Or snorted we in the seven sleepers den?
> > . . .
>
> At this we cease reading as students, or as connoisseurs of anthology-pieces, and read on as we read the living. The extraordinary force of originality that made Donne so potent an influence in the seventeenth century makes him now at once for us, without his being the less felt as of his period, contemporary.[11]

Leavis does not hesitate to equate the exemplary originality of Donne's poetry in the poet's own time with that which makes it fresh and vital for the modern reader.[12] On the face of it, this matching of two moments of originality seems an unlikely coincidence, given the four centuries of cultural change that have intervened, yet it lies at the heart of the distinctiveness of the practice we call art. It is not an experience that occurs in spheres other than art; to be thrilled by the originality of Harrison's chronometers is not to feel that the centuries between their creation and our reception have been temporarily dissolved. How can we explain this affront to rationality that is such a familiar feature of our response to works of art?

In attempting to clarify just what happens at these moments, I shall continue to use "originality" to refer to the opening up of new possibilities achieved by the work of art in its own time and accessible via a process of historical reconstruction, reserving "inventiveness" for the quality of innovation which is directly sensed in the present— a somewhat special meaning of these terms on which the rest of this book will elaborate. Whereas the experience of originality in art, as in other fields, is a matter of re-creating the past, artistic inventiveness— unlike inventiveness in science, mathematics, economics, or politics, which is not clearly distinguishable from originality—bridges past and present. An artistic invention is inventive now.[13]

This is not to say that the historical situatedness of the artistic invention is irrelevant. When I respond to the inventiveness of a work of art, I draw on whatever representation of its historical context I have internalized, and this feeds into, and enhances, my response. Accurate historical knowledge is not an indispensable element in that response, however. The enjoyment of art has never been the sole preserve of the historian. I may be mistaken about the originality of a poem I am reading, but I cannot be mistaken about its inventiveness, since inventiveness is always inventiveness *for the reader*. Of course, I may be unable to persuade anyone else of the poem's inventiveness if my response is based on some personal idiosyncrasy, or on a very limited grasp of my cultural context or that within which the poem was created. In such circumstances, however, it is likely that my experience of inventiveness will be jejune and short-lived. A full engagement with the culture at large and with its history is usually required not only for the creation of inventive art but also for an appreciation of its inventiveness.

How does the bridging of past and present that characterizes a response to inventiveness happen? Although Richardson's *Clarissa* was clearly an inventive arrival upon the eighteenth-century European cultural scene, realizing hitherto occluded possibilities, how is it able to maintain that inventiveness today, read within a very different cultural context? How is it that Caravaggio's inventiveness, which had such an impact on Roman culture at the end of the sixteenth century, still shines out from his paintings when they are exhibited alongside those of his contemporaries? These are puzzles that have never had fully satisfactory answers.

The experience of engaging with an inventive work of the past is an encounter with alterity, an alterity that has either in some way survived the passage of time, or, having been for a time culturally accommodated, once more become an effective absence in the present. The starting-point of this experience is the receiver's own idioculture, which is to say, his or her particular incorporation of the cultural frameworks he or she inhabits. Had Leavis spent more time and energy getting to know the Elizabethan lyric poetry that preceded and surrounded the work of John Donne, he might have found that out of a mass of fairly formulaic writing certain poets or poems began to speak with their own distinctive, and inventive, voices—Fulke Greville, perhaps, whom he slights, or Walter Ralegh, whom he does not mention. It was Donne who appealed to Leavis, however, no doubt partly because the modern critic had already absorbed other developments in the writing and reading of poetry in the early part of the twentieth century that encouraged directness of address, verbal ingenuity, and conspicuous intelligence married to intense feeling. The poems in *Songs and Sonets* offered the experience of a singularity that seemed to address him directly, an alterity that resisted complete accommodation, an inventiveness that happened freshly on every reading. The paradoxical experience Leavis is registering —one we are all familiar with—is of recognition and immediacy at the same time as strangeness and newness. Although the reading of poetry in the seventeenth century differed greatly from the activity to which we give the same name in the twenty-first century, it seems likely that Leavis was, as he claimed, responding to the same inventiveness—the same innovations in tone, rhythm, dramatic presentation, and language—that had played at least some part in making Donne's poetry so powerful and influential in its own day.

But this power to cross large temporal gaps is not available to every artistic invention. At any given moment in cultural history, some works of the past convey their inventiveness powerfully to attentive receivers, while others which may have been just as inventive in earlier periods remain dumb. A work may come into being as a challenge to cultural norms, and retain that challenge across the centuries because it is never fully accommodated—which is to say that the culture never adjusts to such an extent that the work's otherness is completely reduced to sameness. Although the term "Rabelaisian" has passed into many languages, *Gargantua and Pantagruel* remains a work that takes new readers by surprise, there being sufficient continuity between the sixteenth-century norms and expectations it challenged and early twenty-first-century ones to produce similar effects.

Another work may quickly lose its inventiveness, or certain aspects of its inventiveness, as the culture changes, and may or may not regain it. We can never recapture the startling effect of the introduction of a second actor on the Athenian tragic stage; indeed, the alterity of Aeschylus's plays for most of us includes their use of *only* two actors. Sylvester's translation of Du Bartas's *Divine Weekes and Workes*, so eye-opening in the seventeenth century, is now a dull expanse of verse, and Salvator Rosa's romantic landscapes seem (and therefore are) much less inventive to twenty-first-century viewers than they were three centuries earlier. The poetry of Donne is itself a case in point, having provided few, if any, nineteenth-century readers with the experience of immediacy which to Leavis in 1936 seemed obvious.

Clearly, chance must play a role in these historical mutations: for every Hopkins or Dickinson found to be a superbly inventive poet after their death there must be many whose time has not, and may never, come. There are, however, always historical reasons why cultural needs and expectations change. These historical modifications occur both in the narrow tradition within which the work is read—the tradition of the love lyric, say—and in much wider areas of social life and human interaction. Thus Wordsworth's *Prelude* has been altered both by changes in the cultural valuation of the epic poem and by a shift in attitudes about the natural environment; its extraordinary displacement of national or universal narrative by personal autobiography is now unlikely to surprise the reader, but its treatment of the relations between humans and their natural surroundings may carry a greater punch than ever before.

The historically conditioned nature of our responses to art does not render them less valid; this would only be the case if there were such a thing as a completely unconditioned response.[14] "Discoveries" or "rediscoveries" of artists of the past can, of course, be quite superficial, based on accidental similarities between the two cultural contexts, and in such cases the newly appreciated works are unlikely to be enjoyed as inventive or to spur fresh inventions. But if the new context relates to the earlier one in more profound ways, new possibilities of inventiveness in works and *oeuvres* (different but not entirely distinct from their original inventiveness) may come into being. This capacity for reinventing invention is at the heart of artistic survival.

One implication of what I am arguing is that in the case of invention, success can bring a kind of failure. When a work or *oeuvre* of great originality appears on the cultural scene, the effect of its alterity, as we have noted, is a shift in shared understandings and expectations. This process of accommodation may mean that in due course it loses some of the inventive power it possessed on its first appearance, and it certainly means that the imitations it is likely to spawn will seem far less powerful than they would have done to an earlier generation. The paintings and collages created by Picasso and Braque in the second decade of the twentieth century cannot have exactly the effect now that they had then, since the otherness they introduced into the world of visual representation produced a shift in the schemata by which we view art (and perhaps the world beyond art) that has lasted until today. This could mean that for some viewers of our own day these once revolutionary works lack inventiveness and singularity, whereas works that were less influential in their time—the paintings of Henri Rousseau, say—might now have a stronger visual charge. (To the historically aware, the *originality* of Cubist works remains undimmed, of course.) On the other hand, it is true to say that the conventions of representation that dominated Western art from the seventeenth to the nineteenth centuries still hold sway over most pictorial depictions, so at least some of the challenge of Cubist work has not evaporated.

But there is more to the experience of inventiveness than this historical seesaw that pushes some work and artists up while it allows others to sink. If I listen attentively to the opening of Haydn's *Creation*, I enjoy its harmonic adventurousness both as originality—that is to say, I hear it against the expectations I have reconstructed through what I know of the music of its time—and as inventiveness, even though my ears are accustomed to music that takes much greater liberties with the tonal system. This is because the music succeeds in conveying its own inventiveness by engaging with and alluding to the system out of which it emerges and which it challenges. My sense of expectations thwarted and doors opening, in other words, is not only a historical fact, but something built into the music. This is not to say that everyone who listens to *The Creation* has the experience I am describing; it clearly requires familiarity with the dodecaphonic tonal structures that underlie most music from Haydn's time to our own, for example, and probably some familiarity with the classical tradition and orchestral music of the West. A listener who has never heard a symphony orchestra before may be struck by the richness and complexity of the sound, but this would clearly be an idiosyncratic response. The issue is not that of "better" and "worse" responses; it is just that works are always received, as well as created, in a culture or cultures that furnish specific materials, conventions, and expectations, and in so doing keep other possibilities at bay.

How invention begets invention

If the work of art can retain or renew its alterity and inventiveness across temporal gaps—if, indeed, this power is what constitutes it as a work of art—it follows that artists can respond inventively to artistic inventions of earlier periods. A poet writing today is as likely to find the *Aeneid* or *The Vanity of Human Wishes* a spur to fresh inventiveness as a poem written last year. This does not mean, however, that in reaching into the past for inspiration the artist loses touch with contemporary culture; on the contrary, it is only in terms of the significance of the earlier work *for* contemporary culture that inventiveness of this kind can occur. The Pre-Raphaelites, as we have noted, were responding very acutely to the conditions of their time in seeking inspiration from *quattrocento* Italy.

Such trans-temporal movements are much rarer outside the sphere of art. One can imagine—just—a scientist finding in Leonardo's note-books a sketch whose significance has never been appreciated, and using it as the basis for a mechanical invention; and it is certainly possible for a present-day philosopher to be spurred to fresh inventive argument by re-reading Aristotle or Spinoza (although it may not always be clear to what degree their works are being read as philosophy and to what extent as literature, in the sense being developed in this book). These events are possible because elements of certain scientific or philosophical works may remain, or, through a process of historical displacement, become, unaccommodated; they are not essentially different from the cases of delayed inventiveness, such as Slutsky and Mendel, mentioned above. Works of art, however, *depend* on their resistance to accommodation across time; and it is through this resistance that they make further artistic invention possible.

In the case of the work of art, complete cultural accommodation would spell the end of the work's existence as art, since it would no longer be received as an other that opens up new possibilities. Let us consider the example of the Earl of Surrey, who may with some justification be regarded as the inventor of two much-used metrical forms in English: Poulter's measure (rhymed couplets of six and seven beats) and iambic pentameter.[15] Poulter's measure became a very popular form in early Elizabethan poetry, but whatever inventiveness it possessed was quite soon lost. Indeed, it is possible to argue, at least with the somewhat dubious benefit of hindsight, that Surrey, even though he was clearly being original in the more limited sense, was not being inventive in devising a meter that merely regularized a common song rhythm—that his creation of poulter's measure, in other words, introduced no alterity into the existing field of English poetry to challenge and change it but merely provided a template for inferior poets to deploy. By contrast, his creation of a regular accentual-syllabic iambic pentameter produced eddies in the prevailing comprehension of language and speech that made it possible for Sidney after him to explore the tensions between regular meter and the variations of the spoken voice, and Donne and Shakespeare in turn to use Sidney's verse as a springboard to fresh rhythmic developments. The new departures could not, of course, have been predicted from the invention that made them possible—if they could, they would not themselves have been (and continue to be) inventive.[16]

Cultural distance

We have been considering the cultural distance produced by the passage of time, but in our encounters with works of art we also frequently find ourselves being made aware of the differences between simultaneously existing cultural formations. Cultural difference of this kind can operate in a variety of ways. If a reader of José Saramago's fiction in English translations were to find it as compellingly inventive as a Portuguese reader might the original, this would probably be not only because of the skill of the translator but also because of a large degree of overlap between the governing cultural conditions and linguistic norms of contemporary Portugal and Britain. A contemporary work of Korean literature in English translation, however inventive in its own location, may not be so for the English reader, belonging as it does to a quite different cultural tradition. If it *does* move and delight such a reader, rather than just appearing very strange, this may be a sign of the globalization that has diminished cultural differences that were once marked or, alternatively, it may be that the work has a quite distinct kind of inventiveness in its new context, just as an older work in one's own language may be inventive today in ways that could not have been foreseen when it was written. As we noted earlier in discussing such temporal shifts, however, there is always the danger that cross-cultural appreciation may be based on superficial similarities between the two contexts—in which case, the work is unlikely to be received as inventive (in the full sense) in its new domain.

As with the art of the past of my own culture, diligent study might put me in the position of appreciating the originality of a contemporary (or for that matter an ancient) work from a very different culture—that is to say, its significant departures from its predecessors within the culture—and this would be likely to enhance my pleasure in it. But only if I find a way of absorbing the nuances of the other cultural matrix—which might entail living in another place for a considerable period —will I be able to enjoy to the full the inventiveness that the work has in its original context. Because of this possibility of becoming intimately acquainted with another culture, cross-cultural engagement of this kind is achievable in a way that trans-temporal engagement, at least across a generation or two, is not.[17] Of course, within this schematic picture there are many variations and blurrings: artists who work in more than one culture at a time, readers, listeners, and viewers who do the same, works of art that introduce one cultural register into another, and multiple processes of absorption and transformation. The huge impact on the Western cultural scene of recent writing from the former European colonies—an impact which renders the opposition "Western"/"non-Western" highly problematic—is one example of the productiveness of such movements across space.

In all these cases, we are likely to be aware of the work's origin at a distant time or place (or both), and this awareness is itself an inescapable part of our response, quite apart from any particular knowledge we might have about the circumstances of its creation.[18] The same is true of any marked cultural distance that operates across space rather than time. However, like a sense of a work's originality in its time, a sense of its pastness or cultural distance is not part of what makes it *literary*; we respond in a similar fashion to many kinds of artifact—an ancient kitchen utensil redolent of different culinary practices, for instance, or a pair of uncomfortable-looking shoes from a far-away country.

It will be clear that we need to make a distinction between the art of one's own time and place and that which is distant in either or both these respects. If I find inventiveness in a work created last week by an artist working within the culture I call my own, this means that it has succeeded, for me at least, in exploiting the potential of the cultural materials we share (including their relation to the social, economic, and political realities of our time) to introduce otherness into our world and thus to open up fresh possibilities for further inventiveness. By contrast, if I find inventiveness in a work created within a culture that I do *not* call my own, the experience is colored by the considerations discussed above—by the sense of the past or of spatial separation, by a countering sense of trans-historical or trans-geographical continuity (which, in giving the work the power to cross distance, can function to enhance immediacy), and by such awareness as I may have of its originality within its own time and place.

We should not, however, make an absolute distinction between the contemporary artwork and the artwork of the past, nor between that of a geographical and cultural "here" and "there." The artwork to which I respond *always* speaks to me of a foreign country and a distant past (or future). Even a just-published novel which deals with the city in which I live and the class of which I am a member reaches me through a web of linguistic, generic, ethical, social, political, and other assumptions and codes that are not entirely my own. In reading such a book, I am traversing cultural distance, I am opening my own idioculture to possible alteration by an artifact that may share many of my assumptions, but never all of them.

Of course, it is possible to read a work of the past under the misapprehension that it has just been written (this is particularly likely to happen with modern translations of older works), or a work of a different culture thinking it comes from one's own (again, distance is often decreased by translations), and in such cases we respond to the work's inventiveness—if, that is, we do find it inventive—without finding the experience colored by an awareness of pastness or cultural distance. (We may even, mistakenly, attribute originality to it.) Conversely, as Eliot insisted in "Tradition and the Individual Talent" (a work strongly informed by a sense of the time-traversing powers of art), our response to a contemporary work of art is affected by our awareness of the works of the past, and especially works with which it shares a genre or other significant characteristics. Eliot also pointed out that those works of the past change their meaning for us as we engage with their successors—but this is because in responding to any inventive work we are altering our understanding, however minimally, of all the other works we have internalized or will encounter thereafter. My sense of Paul Muldoon's great elegy for Mary Farl Powers changes if I re-read it after getting to know Bion's lament for Adonis, but this reading of Bion is already affected by my knowledge of Muldoon.[19]

In the case of works we find inventive in ways their original audiences, distant from us in time or space, did not, we cannot appeal to a continuity of cultural context. To understand how this kind of invention can happen, we need to return to our earlier discussion of the breakdown of the old that allows otherness to emerge. For a work from a different period or place inventively to introduce otherness into a cultural matrix it is not enough for it simply to impinge on that matrix from outside; any change that such a conjunction produced would be of a predictable and mechanical kind. The reduplication of Celtic intertwined animals as motifs for modern interior decoration does not involve an inventive relation to the original works of art. It is only if the external pressure operates in conjunction with some potential fracture or site of tension within the culture that the conditions exist for the emergence of inventive alterity. When Japan was opened to the West its art had a much more than superficial impact on nineteenth-century European culture; Manet, Degas, and Whistler were among those who responded inventively to the visual alterity of Japanese prints, for instance. That this could happen tells us something about European culture at the time—Japanese art would have had a very different effect (and perhaps very little effect at all) a century earlier. Similarly, what we think of as the rediscovery of Vermeer and Donne in the twentieth century can also be understood as the result of a cultural mutation that made it possible for their paintings and poems to have an impact, as irruptions of alterity, once more. Just as we cannot predict the future of art, so we cannot know in advance which authors and works will come to be inventive— and these facts are both central to what art is.

Inventive language and the literary event   4

Verbal invention

The word "invention" is likely to conjure up images of steam engines or electric light bulbs, though it has a common musical use as well, as in Bach's *Two-Part Inventions*. It is rarely used with reference to purely verbal objects, even if "inventive" and "inventiveness" are part of the standard vocabulary of literary criticism. I trust, however, that it will be clear from the previous chapter why I am extending its use to the verbal field. Inventions employing words take many forms, not just that of the literary work. We can point to philosophical arguments, historical descriptions, or reports of scientific experiments that, when they appear, cannot be accounted for or understood in terms of existing norms, and in being received and accommodated bring about permanent changes in those norms. (We noted above that no sharp distinction exists between originality and inventiveness in these fields.) My focus in this chapter will first be on verbal but not necessarily literary inventions, and then on what it is that makes possible the literary invention. I shall not attempt to broaden the argument to non-verbal invention and the non-verbal arts, other than by way of the occasional hint of what might be entailed in an extrapolation of the argument to this wider realm.

As we have seen, to call the process whereby an inventive artifact comes into the world an *act* is to misrepresent it; it is as much an event that happens to the inventor, and to the culture within which the invention takes place, as it is a willed action of a conscious individual. To succeed in writing a work that is genuinely original, and does more than extend existing norms, is to introduce into the cultural matrix a germ, a foreign body, that cannot be accounted for by its existing codes and practices. This is achieved not just by fashioning into a new shape the materials at hand—in literature these materials include the rules and regularities that govern its forms and its operation as well as its sonic, rhythmic, and graphic properties; in philosophy these are ideas[1]—but, more importantly, by destabilizing them, heightening their internal inconsistencies and ambiguities, exaggerating their proclivities, and exploiting their gaps and tensions, in such a way as to allow the otherness implicit in these materials—the otherness they exclude in order to be what they are—to make itself explicit. Like all inventions, verbal inventions depend on their reception for their existence. The primary modes of reception are of course reading and hearing, and I shall use "reading" to include both of these, except when it is appropriate to make a distinction between them.

Language as event

If inventiveness and singularity are to be found in many different fields, and if even the textual field includes several kinds of invention, what is the specificity of the *literary* invention? Although we cannot expect to arrive at a final and exhaustive answer to this question—a defining characteristic of literature is that it remains open to reinterpretation— we can elaborate some of the most important features of the literary as they manifest themselves at present. In order to do this, we need first to examine the operation of language as signification, the operation upon which literature builds in a way that is different from other modes of verbal invention.

The notion of the "event," which we have already seen to be crucial to invention, is also an important element in the notion of the "sign," though many discussions of signification ignore this dimension. The letter *p*, while it has an abstract existence as a collective agreement about a certain configuration of visible material in relation to a set of other configurations, a neuro-psychological existence in the brains of those who recognize it, and a physical existence on thousands of pages, computer screens, and other surfaces, functions as a sign in the fullest sense only when an event of recognition, usually coupled with an event of combination and an event of comprehension, takes place.[2] We identify, that is to say, the object before us—the colored shape on the billboard, for example—as a "token" corresponding to a "type" with which we are already familiar. And this identification includes the acknowledgment of purposiveness: what we are seeing is not a random scratch or a piece of driftwood that, as we would say, "looks like a *p*" but a shape that some mind (perhaps a long way back in a chain of production) *intended* to look like, or more simply to be, a *p*.[3] This is exactly the same process that occurs when, say, in looking at a heap of rocks I notice a piece of egg-and-dart molding: I am not making a judgment about the closeness of the shapes I see to a particular classical form of architectural decoration, rather, I am making the claim that at some point in the past someone carved the stone with the intention of producing what we now call "egg-and-dart molding." (The fact that the perceiver in such cases can always be mistaken indicates that what is at issue here is not historical truth but the nature of the event of "recognition" itself.)

Something similar could be said of the phoneme /p/ in the domain of sound, except that its physical existence *already* depends on an event. Even if it is a recorded phoneme, its physical correlate in the form of grooves or magnetized particles remains dumb until the event of its translation into hearable sound. This remains true when the sound is digitized and the physical medium is an electromagnetic wave or a stream of photons. However, the sound-event does not become a sign-event unless recognition (which, it should now be clear, means the recognition—or more strictly, the ascription—of an underlying purposiveness) takes place. And similarly for words and sentences.

What if we move from the sentence to the text, the series of sentences produced or perceived as a set with some kind of coherence and hence a beginning and an end: a newspaper article, an anecdote, a biography, a manual, a poem?[4] Here the reader or hearer builds on the recognition and comprehension of smaller units to make judgments about the meaning of the larger unit, again on the assumed basis of purposiveness and in relation to existing norms for the genre in question. We can still refer to this process as an event, though it will be obvious that it is a complex event itself made up of hierarchically arranged events (often including shorter texts) whose boundaries are often weak and porous. The event here—whether of writing, uttering, reading, or hearing—may be discontinuous and may involve repetitions and corrections, and so may lack the purity that we usually associate with the term, but this does not prevent eventness from being central to an understanding of the verbal text.

As we move up the scale from the smallest units of language to larger and larger ones, the opportunities for deviation from existing norms increase while the affront to the interpreting mind produced by deviation decreases: one rarely comes across made-up letters or phonemes, and they are very difficult to make sense of (the unpronounceable "sigla" of *Finnegans Wake* are a case in point); the creation of new words occasionally occurs, though it is easy to slide from fruitful extension of meaning to loss of meaning (as *Finnegans Wake* also amply demonstrates); creativity in the production of sentences is very common, and is much less challenging to the interpreter; and entire texts offer boundless opportunities for innovation, requiring marked deviations from generic conventions to produce strong effects.

The effect of linguistic innovation may be merely blockage or blankness, a shutting-down of the interpretive mechanism, an experience of baffled perplexity that takes the reader or hearer nowhere. It may be a simple recasting of existing rules to allow for a limited number of new possibilities. Or it may be a temporary remaking of norms in a manner that does not involve straightforward extension or extrapolation, and that produces not an interpretation but something like an experience of meaning *in process*, of "meaning" understood as a participle of the verb "to mean" rather than as a noun—as the experience of an event, in short. The possibilities of this kind of creativity are, of course, limitless, since every rule, every norm, every habit, every expectation involved in the use of language can be stretched, twisted, cited, thwarted, or exaggerated, and in multiply varied combinations with one another. It can manifest itself as a striking challenge to comprehension or as the slightest experience of unfamiliarity haunting the familiar. It can be felt as easily in a work written three centuries ago as in one that is hot off the press, as readily in an old favorite being re-read yet again as in a first-time encounter. When language is subjected to *this* kind of innovation, it seems apt to call it literary invention.

The literary event

Not every linguistic innovation that requires a reformulation of existing norms, therefore, is a literary invention; most, in fact, are not. One could program a computer to produce millions of linguistic items that deviate from the rules of English in this way without a single one being apprehensible as a literary work. It is only when the event of this reformulation is experienced by the reader (who is, in the first instance, the writer reading or articulating the words as they emerge) *as an event,* an event which opens new possibilities of meaning and feeling (understood as verbs), or, more accurately, the event *of such opening,* that we can speak of the literary. The predilections and conventions by means of which most events of comprehension occur are challenged and recast, not merely as automatic extensions but as invitations to alterity, and thus to modes of mental processing, ideas and emotions, or conceptual possibilities that had hitherto been impossible—impossible because the status quo (cognitive, affective, ethical) depended on their exclusion. This process of initiation, this movement into the unknown, is experienced as something that *happens to* the reader in the course of a committed and attentive reading.

This is what a literary work "is": an act, an event, of reading, never entirely separable from the act-event (or acts-events) of writing that brought it into being as a potentially readable text, never entirely insulated from the contingencies of the history into which it is projected and within which it is read. The statement that a work is not an object but an event may be a truism, but it is a truism whose implications have generally been resisted. In spite of a long history of critiques of the notion of literature as constative—Benjamin sums up a whole tradition when he says that the essential quality of the literary work "is not statement or the imparting of information"[5]—surprisingly few of our readings acknowledge this in practice. We still talk about "structure" and "meaning," and ask what a work is "about," in a manner that suggests a static object, transcending time, permanently available for our inspection.

It will be obvious that my use of "literary" and "literature" here does not accord with some of the commonly accepted meanings of these terms. I employ the words to designate the potential possessed by a body of texts for a certain effectivity, a potential realized differently—or not at all—in different times and places. (Since the literariness of any given text may always emerge in the future if it has not done so in the past, this is a body with no determined limits.) Literature has of course frequently been regarded as having, and perhaps being partly defined by, certain effects on its readers: humanizing them, broadening their minds, alerting them to linguistic niceties, enlarging their sympathies, undermining their covert ideological assumptions, and so forth.

This is not the kind of effectivity of which I am speaking. Literary works undoubtedly may have any of these effects, and a good number of others, but when they do, it is not as a direct result of their being *literary*, though it may be as a result of one part of the author's intentions (since writers of literary works usually have several simultaneous aims).

The effects of the literariness of certain linguistic works (whether or not they are conventionally classified as "literature") are not predictable and do not arise from planning, and although artistic inventiveness may play a crucial role in the ethical status of a culture—since a culture that does not continually find ways of opening itself to the excluded other on which it depends can hardly be said to be ethical—there can be no guarantee that the alterity brought into the world by a particular literary or other artistic work will be beneficial.[6] In the worst case, the introduction of alterity could destroy a culture. This is the risk involved in any welcoming of the other. (Of course, longstanding laws and customs usually continue to play a part in limiting potential damage and safeguarding traditional values, though even they can be disabled or discredited by the irruption of the other.)

Another familiar position is that *all* valorization of literature is merely ideological, and that we should apply the term "literature" in a value-free manner to any textual production of an imaginative or fictional character. There is nothing inherently wrong with such a position: it is one possibility allowed for by our current varied and inconsistent use of the word "literature." My quarrel with this more general use of the term is that accepting it here would make it harder to find a word or phrase for the narrower category I am interested in, and which corresponds, at least roughly speaking, to another possibility allowed for by current usage. Phrases like "genuine literature" or "real literature" would only exacerbate the problem. Perhaps the best solution, if one wants to maintain the widest sense of the term, would be to distinguish between "literature in general" and "inventive literature," and if the reader wishes to give this gloss to the word in what follows, he or she is welcome to do so.

It will also be evident that the "literary" in the somewhat specialized sense in which I am using the term is not confined to the recognized institution of literature (which of course frequently changes its boundaries); nor is it the case that everything classified at a particular historical juncture as "literature" embodies, or continues to embody, the literary.

The term has had a variety of meanings that are no longer current —"book-learning" from the fourteenth century to the eighteenth, "writing in any genre reaching a polite standard" from the eighteenth century into the nineteenth[7]—and there are contemporary meanings that have little connection with our topic, as in "the literature on genetic modification" or "the campaign literature." The label "literature" has been applied to pot-boilers or politically commanded endeavors that lack the effectivity I have mentioned, and withheld from other works— Engels's *Condition of the English Working Class* or Freud's *Interpretation of Dreams*, might be examples—that could be said to possess it.

Nevertheless, the agreed-upon category of literature as it has emerged in the last two centuries remains the major repository of the literary, and when we call a philosophical or historical work "literary" it is its affiliation to the body of works historically acknowledged as literature to which we are drawing attention. I see no reason to proscribe the retrospective application of this category to periods before its emergence around the end of the eighteenth century, as long as this is done with due caution; it would be merely pedantic to insist on the term "poetry" (as the nearest equivalent) when discussing the fictional prose of Sidney or Swift. Nor should the designation "literature" be construed as applying only to the productions of "high" or "elite" culture: inventive literary works, like inventive films or inventive songs, may be very popular indeed. Since inventiveness is an attribute of the experience of reading, it is not strictly possible to judge certain works as being "more inventive" than others; but the phrase is meaningful if understood as shorthand for "more likely to be experienced as inventive at a particular historical moment" (and possibly "for a particular group").

Although literary inventiveness is something that is experienced only by individuals, it is the culture at large that determines whether this or that work is literary. A significant number of a work's readers must acknowledge a work's inventiveness before it can be called "literary" from a cultural or institutional perspective. There is often disagreement about this question: a given work may be received as literary by some readers, and not by others. And although it is true to say that within a given culture at a given time there will be a certain body of works that are widely received as literary, the slightest acquaintance with literary history shows that it is a far from stable category. In fact, one of the ways in which a literary work can be inventive is by operating at the unstable limits of the literary, and reinventing the category itself. Defoe's achievement could be thought of in these terms, and so, in a very different mode, could Mallarmé's. Nor can we impose in advance any limit on these reinventions of the category: there can be no guarantee that the future will have a place for the literary.

Singularity 5

The event of singularity

Inseparable from the notions of invention and alterity is, as we have had many occasions to observe, the notion of *singularity*. The other, the unprecedented, hitherto unimaginable disposition of cultural materials that comes into being in the event of invention, is always singular, although that singularity can be experienced only as a process of adjustment in norms and habits whereby it is recognized, affirmed, and, at least partially and temporarily, accommodated. But what, in this scenario, is singularity? The word has been used in many ways in literary and philosophical discussions, and it is important to be as clear as possible about its meaning here.[1] The singularity of a cultural object consists in its difference from all other such objects, not simply as a particular manifestation of general rules but as a peculiar nexus within the culture that is perceived as resisting or exceeding all pre-existing general determinations. Singularity, that is to say, is generated not by a core of irreducible materiality or vein of sheer contingency to which the cultural frameworks we use cannot penetrate but by a configuration of general properties that, in constituting the entity (as it exists in a particular time and place), go beyond the possibilities pre-programmed by a culture's norms, the norms with which its members are familiar and through which most cultural products are understood. Singularity is not *pure*: it is constitutively impure, always open to contamination, grafting, accidents, reinterpretation, and recontextualization. Nor is it inimitable: on the contrary, it is eminently imitable, and may give rise to a host of imitations.

Strictly speaking, therefore, singularity, like alterity and inventiveness, is not a property but an event, the event of singularizing which takes place in reception: it does not occur outside the responses of those who encounter and thereby constitute it. It is produced, not given in advance; and its emergence is also the beginning of its erosion, as it brings about the cultural changes necessary to accommodate it. Singularity is not the same as autonomy, particularity, identity, contingency, or specificity; nor is it to be equated with "uniqueness," a word which I shall employ to refer to an entity which is unlike all other entities *without* being inventive in its difference—which is to say, without introducing otherness into the sphere of the same. A work that is unique but not singular is one that may be wholly comprehended within the norms of the culture: indeed, it is the process of comprehension—the registering of its particular configuration of familiar laws—that discloses its uniqueness.

Singularity has also always been valued and enjoyed in Western art, even though in certain periods the idea of singularity was frowned upon.[2] Its opposite, for which there are many names (triteness, imitativeness, banality, hackwork, cliché, stereotype), has always been seen as a mark of weakness and a cause of boredom and irritation. To value singularity is not, however, to value what Benjamin called the "aura" of the specific, unique art-object; singularity can inhere as much in a photograph reproduced a million times as in the colored plaster of Leonardo's "Last Supper" in the refectory of the monastery of Santa Maria delle Grazie. Singularity may also inhere in a group of works or an entire *oeuvre*: we have already discussed the experience of being addressed directly by an immediately recognizable voice when an author's characteristic inventiveness has become familiar. In this respect (we shall come to others later) singularity functions like a signature. It would be more accurate, in fact, to describe singularity as *nested*: that of the work (or sometimes a part of the work; the speech of a character, for instance) within that of the *oeuvre* (or sometimes a part of the *oeuvre*, like the "late works") within that of the period or artistic movement. The experience of singularity is the experience of these nested singularities. Nor does the inventive singularity of the artwork simply reside in the historical past, available for retrospective enjoyment; as I have argued, it bridges, in a way that is not easy to explain, past and present.

The singularity of the literary work: an example

The title of this book refers not only to the distinctiveness and surprisingness of the body of texts and the cultural practice that we understand by that name; it is meant also to underline the importance of a certain kind of specificity in our sense of the individual work of literature. Literary singularity may be said to derive from—though it is much more than—the *verbal particularity* of the work: specific words in a specific arrangement (which may include spatial arrangement on the page or the use of pauses and other articulating devices in oral delivery). This verbal sequence exists as a literary work only in a reading; singularity, to say it again, has to be understood, like alterity and invention, as an event.

Here is a poem by William Blake we all know:

The Sick Rose

O rose, thou art sick.
The invisible worm,
That flies in the night
In the howling storm,

Has found out thy bed
Of crimson joy:
And his dark secret love
Does thy life destroy.[3]

This arrangement of thirty-four words is unique in the way that the identity of any one-off cultural artifact is unique. It constitutes a linguistic text that is different from every other linguistic text, which is only to say that these words in this order set out in this way will always constitute this poem. A Pierre Menard writing these words in the twentieth century is still writing, in a straightforward sense, the same poem; any metaphysical or deconstructive speculation on the difference it makes to write the same words in a different century is wholly dependent upon the certainty of the initial identification.[4]

Another way of putting this is that the differences observable in the variety of manifestations of this poem—whether it be printed, written, spoken, sung, illuminated, or recorded, and in whatever font, style of handwriting, delivery, musical setting, mode of decoration, or type of transcription—are treated as ignorable for the purposes of identifying the poem as Blake's "Sick Rose"; all the different manifestations, that is, are types of a single token (even though a particular mode of presentation may have a strong impact on responses to the poem). Of course, there is an obscure border area, where there would be disagreements about whether we have before us the "same" poem or not: authorial variants, translations, rewritings, mis-transcriptions, and fragments, and so on. (I discuss translations and imitations in a later section of this chapter.) What these uncertainties indicate is that the identity of the poem is not secure, walled-up in itself, but open to its outside and open to history, sustained only by a certain cultural vigilance or even violence. These complications, however, operate in all instances of identity and all types of signification.

A fuller sense of the uniqueness of this poem, as a poem rather than simply a verbal arrangement, is given by an appreciation of its specific employment of the possibilities offered by the literary tradition and the wider cultural context: the distinctive combination, for instance, of a nursery-rhyme-like rhythm with sexual imagery, or the exploitation of the genre of the apostrophe, or the deployment of syntax to achieve an unrelenting onward drive that climaxes on a single powerful word. An appreciation of the poem's uniqueness in this sense depends not just on a knowledge of the English language and its stylistic possibilities but also on familiarity with the traditions within which the poem was written, and may also be enhanced by an awareness of the specific historical and biographical context of its creation. In the case of "The Sick Rose," knowledge of its original format—as an illuminated page in Blake's *Songs of Experience*—enhances an appreciation of its distinctiveness, as does familiarity with the traditions of popular four-beat verse such as the ballad, the hymn, and the nursery-rhyme. An acquaintance with the other poems in *Songs of Experience* and with the earlier collection to which this one was added, *Songs of Innocence* (and within this collection its contrary poem, "The Blossom"), gives a further substance to the reader's awareness of its particularity, and the same is true of an acquaintance with other poems and prose writings by Blake, and by his contemporaries and predecessors.

The literary object's uniqueness does not transcend history, however: the features that constitute "The Sick Rose" as a poem with a certain richness and density at the beginning of the twenty-first century are different from those that constituted it at the beginning of the nineteenth century. This is to say that, while it remains the same poem, the grounds of its uniqueness have continued to change—in fact, only through this process of constant and endless change has it remained the same. Again, this is a feature of all semiotic identity.

What I am calling the singularity of the poem, although it depends upon an appreciation of its uniqueness and therefore of the properties I have enumerated, is not to be equated with them. A literary work is singular not just in the sense that it is the only one to use these words in this order, or this syllabic pattern in this stanza-form: that would make singularity very cheap, as well as easy to analyze and to bring within the sphere of the same. One way of thinking of singularity is as the *demand* that this specific collocation of words, allusions, and cultural references makes on me in the event of my reading, here and now, as a member of the culture to whom these codes are familiar. Singularity exists, or rather *occurs*, in the experience of the reader (including the writer-as-reader), understood not as a psychological subject (though singularity has its psychological effects) but as the repository of what I have termed an idioculture, an individual version of the cultural ensemble by which he or she has been fashioned as a subject with assumptions, predispositions, and expectations.

Not only is the poem, registered in the reader's experience of it, different from every other poem he or she has encountered, but that difference cannot be explained, nor that singularity exhausted, by an exposition, however full, of the dissimilarities and similarities that constitute its uniqueness and richness as a cultural object. The experience of singularity involves an apprehension of *otherness*, registered in the event of its apprehension, that is to say, in the mental and emotional opening that it produces. Singularity is, as I have stressed, also inseparable from *inventiveness*. The experience I am describing involves an appreciation, a living-through, of the invention that makes the work not just different but a creative re-imagination of cultural materials.

The singularity of the literary work, then, does not lie in any essence of the work, any inalterable and ineffable core or kernel. An unchanging, essential uniqueness would in fact be unreadable and imperceptible, since it would not be open to any of the codes and processes by which we read and perceive. Nor is it a matter of firm boundaries or organic unity. Perceived unity—created, for example, by Blake's use of a single sentence over seven lines in "The Sick Rose," his deployment of a single four-by-four metrical structure divided into eight two-beat lines and bound into four four-beat units by an *aabb* rhyme-scheme,[5] the movement from the subject "worm" to the two verbs enclosing the second stanza in a chiasmic progression, the strong closure on the last word—may constitute an important part of the reader's response to and enjoyment of a literary work, but it does not in itself produce singularity. Singularity arises from the work's constitution *as a set of active relations*, put in play in the reading, that never settle into a fixed configuration. These active relations can produce a sense of multiple voices addressed to multiple audiences, so much so that the "I" who reads may momentarily lose its coherence.

Because the singularity of "The Sick Rose" inheres in readings of the poem, each singular in a different way, it cannot be demonstrated in the way that its unity, its symbolism, or its use of meter can be. I can bear imperfect witness to its singularity—its singularity for me, here, now—by describing a little of what happens when I read it on the occasion of writing this chapter, although any such description has to take its chances with readers in the same way that a literary work does. What I am giving an account of is not the operation of the work's singularity as such but the reflex of that operation in my experience; if I succeed in conveying its singularity it will be because my description, read in conjunction with the poem, generates in turn an event of singularity for the reader. This is how much successful criticism works.

For me, now, the poem's singularity arises in part from the combined experience, as the single syntactic unit unfolds and draws me on, of movements of enclosure and movements of opening. The sentence presents me with a series of words and phrases going beyond (while it never leaves behind) the everyday garden scene on an uncontrollable journey through the resources of the culture and, though I can only guess at this, the unconscious. Word after word resonates through a variety of registers; to mention just a few, "sick" (ill, sick with love, sick at heart), "invisible" (ghostly, minute, immaterial, repressed, metaphysical), "night" (literal and spiritual darkness, evil, unseen depths), "howling" (noise of wind, of grief, of terror, of animal rage or despair), "crimson" (rose-red, intense, blood-like, sexual). The result of this opening out of meaning is that even a word like "worm" acquires a density of suggestiveness that moves well beyond its apparent sense ("a maggot, grub, or caterpillar, esp. one that feeds on and destroys flesh, fruit, leaves, cereals, textile fabrics, and the like," to cite the *OED*) to archaic senses ("serpent, snake, dragon") and figurative uses ("one of the pains of Hell," "the gnawing of remorse," the body as "worm's meat"), to myth (the Garden of Eden, the loathly worm of the ballad tradition) and phallic suggestiveness. Further intensifying these multiplying significations is an awareness that in the late eighteenth century many of them would have been more present in daily usage, and that the oral tradition on which the poem draws would have been a familiar element of cultural experience. These potential meanings are all part of the poem's specificity, and would figure in any account of its uniqueness; its singularity lies in the *activation* of these unfurling meanings, in the experience—unlike that induced by any other literary work I have read— of increasing semantic depth and density.

The poem's occurrence as apostrophe is part of its singular happening, too. It positions the reader both as addresser and addressee: seeing the rose through the eyes of the speaker and sharing his or her undecidable, yet powerful, feelings about it (horror? gloating? pity? exultation?), and at the same time occupying the same place as the rose, indicted, exposed, destroyed. The nursery-rhyme rhythm with its strong beats and simple rhyme-scheme also plays a part in the double movement that carries the reader through the poem, both pulling back from the further reaches of symbolism by its insistence on artlessness and yet at the same time increasing the symbolic drive by hinting at the depths below the apparently simple surface of childhood language and feeling. The alterity through which the poem challenges cultural norms (its disruption, for instance, of the web of associations constituting the idea of the nursery rhyme or the rose or love) is both an external and an internal irruption: the occulted recesses of my own weave of thought-patterns and emotional dispositions are also those of the culture that has formed me.

The simplicity of the strongly articulated phrasal movement contributes to this experience. The arresting initial statement, "O rose, thou art sick."—one line, two beats—is followed, after a pregnant pause, by an extension that takes up the seven remaining lines.[6] This extended elaboration of the opening line is made up of three lines of anticipation, followed by the stanza break which further heightens the tension, and then a four-line arrival. And those three lines of anticipation form a crescendo of intensity—"The invisible worm, / That flies in the night / In the howling storm,"—while the stanza of arrival varies the 1:3 balance of the first stanza by taking the reader through two climactic statements of equal length: "Has found out thy bed / Of crimson joy: / / And his dark secret love / Does thy life destroy." The final two lines, phrasally no more than an extension of the previous statement, work semantically to explode the thus far barely contained nursery-rhyme narrative into the most adult, and most terrible, of scenarios.

There is a great deal more that could be said about the singularity of this poem, but what I wish to establish here is the *eventness* of that singularity (though my summary is, inevitably, more of a commentary than an inventive response to the event of the poem). Because it happens as an event, singularity is not fixed; if I read the poem tomorrow, I will experience its singularity differently. Further information about the conditions under which Blake wrote the poem, about the literary and popular traditions on which he was drawing, about the connotations of words current in his time, may all feed into the singularity I both create and undergo when I next read it. In the chapters to come we shall elaborate this rather sketchy account of literary singularity by elaborating on questions of reading and performance, on the element of self-distancing that makes the poem a literary work and not only a narrative or descriptive account.

Before moving on, however, we should note that for many nineteenth-century readers, Blake's poem may well have been unique but not singular—that is to say, a curiosity unlike anything else they had ever read but not inventive in the full sense. To take another example of this distinction: in notoriously finding fault with Milton's poetic language T. S. Eliot was perhaps responding to its uniqueness but not its singularity—he registered its remarkable difference from the writing of all other poets, but was not able to respond to its alterity and inventiveness.[7] Nor did he experience it as original (in the sense still of Kant's "exemplary originality"): he saw that it reshaped linguistic possibilities in the seventeenth century and thus spawned imitations, but not how it revitalized poetic language and helped to spur the fresh inventiveness of Wordsworth and Keats. A work we find merely bizarre or willfully eccentric will register as unique, but unless we are able to receive its uniqueness as a creative contribution to our own thinking and feeling it will not convey the pleasure and excitement that usually accompany the apprehending of inventiveness; it will not, in short, happen as an event but will remain resolutely an object. It will not, therefore, impinge upon us as an other, requiring a recasting of our habits and expectations, but merely as a text different from other texts.

The distinctiveness of poetry

Is poetry a definably distinctive type of literature? Much ink has been spilled on this question, and it is evident that if what is implied are intrinsic markers or clear-cut boundaries the answer is no. Just as the borderline between the literary and the non-literary is shifting and porous, so is the borderline between what is called "poetry" and what is not. Several different variables map onto this distinction, and isolating one will always be a somewhat artificial act. And even if we simplify the issue by focusing on one variable, it will be more helpful to think in terms of the degree to which any literary work is poetic, or invites the kind of response we normally accord to poetry, rather than imagining that we can distinguish absolutely between poems and non-poems.

Accepting these caveats, we may isolate one important factor in poetry or the poetic: the verbal singularity that is performed by the reader includes *a sense of its real-time unfolding*. That is to say, what is performed is not just a linear sequence of specific words, but their happening in an experience of temporality. In order to perform a poem in real time I need to read it aloud, or with a sub-vocal articulation that retains the temporal relations of the words and sentences. If a line seems to invite, by its arrangement of stresses or by its sense, a particularly slow or particularly rapid reading, this becomes part of its meaning; when I pause, this lapse of time enters the poetic experience. On the other hand, in reading a novel it makes little difference to my sense of the work whether I read the sentences slowly or fast, whether I make a short or a long pause between paragraphs; as long as the sentences can be processed, as long as the pause can register a break, they achieve their purpose. To the extent that these decisions *do* make a difference, I am reading the novel as poetry.

I do not mean to suggest that poetry depends on actual, measurable time elapsed in the reading, or that a stop-watch would be a useful tool in poetic criticism. A sense of real-time unfolding is produced in part by actual temporal relations, it is true, but more importantly by the linguistic features that demand particular actions on the part of the speech-organs. Thus, for example, an arrangement of stressed and unstressed syllables in combination with syntactic phrasing can produce the temporal, somatic experience of a metrical rhythm, by requiring a particular physical articulation and harnessing a familiar pattern of regular verse. (The four-by-four movement of Blake's "Sick Rose" is a simple but powerful example.) This metrical pattern will be perceived as a molding of time into equivalent units, marked by an alternation of tension and relaxation, beats and offbeats, even when the actual temporal durations of the syllables in a reading vary greatly. Time is controlled and organized by the poem's language—above all by its management of rhythm—and to read a poem as a poem is to experience this controlling activity, not to measure off temporal units.

My argument should not be taken to imply that prose literature relies purely on sense; to believe this would be to believe, for instance, that the difference between James's and Hemingway's syntax lies only in the contrasting meanings they convey. Clearly, effects of complexity, of suspense and resolution, of referral back and forward, of the piling-up of implication, and so on, are important resources for the prose writer. The point I am making is that such effects depend not on the experience of real-time unfolding but on linearity, sequentiality, and relations between words and between syntactic and semantic units. Prose literature presents particular words in a particular order, but not words occurring in a controlled experience of time.

It is important to add that works standardly classified as poetry do not have to be read as poetry; a lot of the time we read poems as if they were prose. Some long poems—Southey's *Madoc*, perhaps, or Hardy's *The Dynasts*—are best read as prose, or only intermittently as poetry. Conversely, there are prose works which yield to a "poetic" reading in this sense: much of Dickens, for instance, exploits the sonic and rhythmic properties of English in a manner that can be most fully enjoyed in reading aloud. Prose-poems, too, trouble the categorization that they bridge.

Many poems employ space as an instruction of sorts to the reader, inviting a pause of a certain duration, with larger spaces implying longer pauses. Other visual arrangements can function in parallel ways to influence the reading. Some poets, however, use spatial arrangement to create effects in part by *resisting* the expectation that poems occur in time. Concrete poetry often cannot be read as a temporal sequence; instead the action of the eye in traversing space becomes the active principle of the poem. Spatial poetry is much rarer than temporal poetry, but it remains a legitimate exploration of the physical modalities of language. Thus in poetry as in literature and art more generally, any borderline we attempt to draw becomes a potential challenge for a future inventive practice.

Translation and imitation

If the singularity of the literary work arises from its existence as a series of specific words in a specific arrangement, it may seem that a translation of the work into a different language will result in a completely new literary work, since none of those words survives in the new version. There is a sense in which this is true, and importantly so, for it underlines the distinctiveness of *literary* inventiveness and singularity: other kinds of inventive text—scientific, philosophical, theological, and so on—can be translated without loss of their singular inventiveness (at least to the degree that this inventiveness is not literary). However, there is also a sense in which literary singularity, far from being opposed to translatability, goes hand-in-hand with it.

What is singular about any artwork is its redeployment of the resources of the culture, understood as sets of relations rather than concrete objects; and this redeployment, because it introduces new perspectives and relationships which can be understood as the implementation of new codes and norms, always offers the possibility of imitation, translation, parody, and forgery. The singular work is therefore not merely *available* for translation but is *constituted* in what may be thought of as an unending set of translations—for each new context in which it appears produces a further transformation. Words irrecoverably change their meanings, historical hindsight shifts emphases, generic expectations alter over the centuries, and in multiple other ways the work continually becomes another work for its readers. Whatever these transmutations, we still do not hesitate to think of the novel we read as the "same" novel its author wrote or its earliest readers encountered.

A poem that has been translated into another language has undergone a more extreme version of this necessary process, but not an absolutely different one. We read Milton's translation of Horace's Fifth Ode from Book One as a version of the original, which means that even while we respond to its specific arrangement of specific English words (and therefore as a singular English poem) we complicate that response—especially if we know the Latin text—by reading it as Horace's poem as well. What this helps us to see is that the formula "specific words in a specific arrangement" should not be read as implying an unchanging material object: words and their arrangements are, to say it again, *relations* or *relatings*, and these specificities can be respected even when the material entities themselves undergo transformations. The materiality of the words and their arrangement counts for more in a poem than in a novel, but is still open to modification—most of us do not, for instance, hesitate to pronounce the words of a Renaissance poem as if they belonged to contemporary English.

Translation in the sense of complete transference from one language to another is impossible, then, for the same reason that identical repetition of any work is impossible; but translation as a process of always incomplete transfer of what is literary in a work is part and parcel of the singularity of literature. Inventive singularity is what provokes translation (in all senses) as a creative response, rather than a mechanical rewording. To translate is, of course, to welcome the work as an other into the same, to transform it from the foreign to the familiar; but in so doing, if its otherness and singularity are respected—if, that is, the translation is inventive—the field into which it is welcomed is also transformed in the process.

This insistence on translation does not mean that there is a clear boundary at which a literary work ceases to be itself and becomes something else. Milton prefaced his Horace translation with the words "Rendered almost word for word without rhyme according to the Latin measure, as near as the language will permit," and we have no difficulty in regarding his poem as a version of Horace's—as Milton's response, that is, to the earlier poet's specific verbal arrangement. By contrast, we often read translations of novels without taking any account of the work of the translator; we are not conscious of reading anything other than the words of Balzac or Solzhenitsyn. In between there are many degrees and kinds of translation, which readers with varying proportions of relevant knowledge treat in many different ways. In every case, the work makes a claim as an arrangement of particular words in the language in which we encounter it; what varies is the reading's possible coloring by an awareness of a predecessor text in a different language, as one among many ways in which it may be enriched by the reader's prior knowledge.

One variety of literary translation in the wider sense is imitation, the production of a work that follows the stylistic and generic norms established by another work—a kind of translation into the same language. It may seem that the more imitable a work is, the less inventive, but this is not the case. The generation of imitations is, we have already seen, one sign of a work's inventiveness—although if it spurs nothing but imitations, it cannot be said to be inventive, since its retexturing of the cultural fabric has not opened up new possibilities of invention. (However, we must remember that inventiveness can always emerge retrospectively at a later date.)

Within the domain of imitation there are, again, many types and degrees, from diligent reproduction of characteristic features (which we might think of as a response to the work's uniqueness rather than to its singularity) to inventive reworkings. From classical times to the eighteenth century, imitation of earlier literary works, or *imitatio*, usually meant the latter, and was more often than not combined with (and not clearly distinguished from) translation; thus many of Petrarch's love poems were imitated by English Renaissance poets, and the same is true in the eighteenth century of Horace's Odes and Satires.

Parody is also a form of imitation, in which it is possible to be highly inventive while mimicking another work. We may note that imitation, including parody, is not a meaningful activity in discourses other than literature: one can either bring into being a new theory in the field of physics, for instance, or simply repeat an existing one; it is not possible to imitate someone else's theory. Any imitation that might occur would have to take as its basis the formal features of the original, and this would mean treating it as a literary work.

Thus we see that imitation, like translation, is not opposed to singularity; the singular literary work is singular only by virtue of its translatability and its imitability (as well as its capacity to provoke new and singular responses). Of course there is no such thing as a pure imitation, just as there is no such thing as a complete translation. Literary identity, as we have seen, involves both repetition of what is recognized as "the same" and openness to new contexts and hence to change.

Intimacy and strangeness

In discussing the question of the literary in terms of otherness and singularity, I have tended to stress the element of unfamiliarity, resistance, and difficulty in our reading of works of literature. My approach has perhaps been the dominant one in the Western tradition; it could be said to embrace Aristotle on the appropriate style for poetry, Longinus and the many eighteenth-century and later attempts to develop a theory of the sublime, Vasari's account of distinguished artists, much Romantic criticism, Freud and most of those influenced by him, and a large swathe of modernist and postmodern criticism. Nevertheless, there is also a long tradition of representing literary experience in very different terms, summed up nicely in the title of Wayne Booth's book on the ethics of fiction, *The Company We Keep*. Booth gives several examples of the metaphor of the book or author as friend from the nineteenth and early twentieth centuries (see his Chapter 6, "Implied Authors as Friends and Pretenders"), and it would not be difficult to find equivalent statements from earlier periods.

Some of this anthropomorphic enthusiasm has little to do with literature as such: it has been felt for writers of all kinds of text, and reflects a certain astonishment at the capacity of language to suggest a human personality through the apparently passionless medium of print. But it does serve as a useful reminder of the doubleness of the literary experience. We have seen that the inventive singularity of a work or a body of work may produce a sense of recognition and even intimacy. One of the pleasures of coming to know a singular *oeuvre* well is the feeling of familiarity we obtain when we read a work that has all the hallmarks of the author in question: characteristic ways of handling syntax and rhythm, immediately recognizable similes, well-known devices of plot, and so on.

Let me make it clear once more that the "otherness" I am positing as central to the experience of the literary is neither a mystical ideality nor an inviolable materiality, neither a Platonic Form nor a Kantian *Ding an sich*. The other can emerge only as a version of the familiar, strangely lit, refracted, self-distanced. It arises from the intimate recesses of the cultural web that constitutes subjectivity, which is to say it arises as much from within the subject as from outside it—and in so doing blurs the distinction between that which is "inside" and that which is "outside" the self. The otherness brought into existence by the work of literature need not be disturbing or startling; indeed, for the work to survive it must be, at least in some way, pleasurable—that is to say, it must be sufficiently positive to arouse a desire for repetition. If we could apprehend otherness directly, the shock would indeed be traumatic; but direct apprehension is exactly what is ruled out. What we experience is not the other but the shifts of mental and emotional gear that make it possible for what was other to be apprehended, now ceasing to be, at least momentarily, other. This experience of increased possibilities for thought and feeling is a welcome one, even though the thoughts and feelings themselves may, as in the case of Shakespeare's tragedies or Hardy's late novels, involve discomfort and distress. (It is important to note, however, that otherness can be effective without registering as a conscious experience. We shall return to this point in the following chapter.)

The mental and emotional expansion demanded by the work, therefore, may be extensive and hard to sustain, or it may be very slight, or somewhere in between. The account I have given of artistic invention helps to explain the tradition of the artist as hero or madman, but it also helps to explain the tradition of artist as friend and companion. The work that reassures by its familiar rehearsal of what we already know, if it functions as literature, is likely to demand only a minimal modification of our habitual patterns of thought and feeling, perhaps only the coming-into-consciousness of practices and relations that are usually taken for granted. It is important to realize, too, that the experience is not always one of thinking the hitherto unthinkable: it may be one of capturing in language something already apprehended in some non-verbal way—Pope's "What oft was thought, but ne'er so well expressed." (Of course, such an experience may be an illusion, an instance of *Nachträglichkeit*, produced retrospectively by the successful invention.) There is ample testimony to the power of literary works to offer profound consolation to their readers; this happens when the experience of the work enables the reader to reconceive his or her situation—by, in other words, the changes brought about through the acceptance of that which had been excluded. If a work comforts and reassures by simply confirming prejudices or reasserting truisms according to well-known verbal formulae, however, it cannot be called literature in the sense in which I am using the term.

It is the case, I believe, that some sense of strangeness, mystery, or unfathomability is involved in every encounter with the literary. Even a work one knows well, if it retains its inventiveness, possesses an enigmatic quality; one cannot put one's finger on the sources of its power, one does not know where its meanings end. Only a work that has lost its inventiveness through over-familiarity, or one that is too formulaic to possess any inventiveness at all, seems wholly knowable, yielding all its meanings up in one go—in which case the experience is not that of closeness and companionship but of boredom. Of course it is possible to read a work one knows well without the kind of openness and attentiveness that allows its alterity to make itself felt (the demands of this mode of reading will be discussed in the next chapter), to read simply for the pleasure of familiarity in a casual or mechanical way. (This mode of enjoyment through familiarity is probably even more common in listening to music, where it is possible to experience pleasure while in a state of complete passivity.) Pleasure of this kind —which is an important aspect of our enjoyment of art—is not easily distinguishable from the more strictly literary pleasure I am attempting, somewhat artificially, to isolate: when I re-read a poem that is an old favorite, I may for the most part just let it re-animate ingrained memory traces, but occasionally find that its singularity strikes me afresh. We all know that feeling, which, if articulated, would be expressed as: "In all the times I've read this work, I've never noticed how . . . " or "I'd totally forgotten just what . . . "

The experience of intimacy that we sometimes have in reading a work for the first time, then, is not a sign that it lacks singularity, inventiveness, and alterity. On the contrary, a sense that the work speaks to my inmost, perhaps secret, being, that it utters thoughts I have long nurtured but never had the power to express, is likely to be an effect not so much of its confirming already distinct and fully configured ideas and preferences but rather of its tapping into deeply rooted elements of my idioculture, precipitating and crystallizing them, bringing some obscured perceptions out of the shadows while discarding others. The singularity of the work thus speaks to my own singularity.

Reading and responding 6

Creative reading

Otherness may be brought into the world, through the event of creation, in a number of fields: in writing, in scientific, mathematical, or philosophical thought, in political practice, and in painting or musical composition, to name just a few possibilities. It may also emerge, as I have already suggested, in responses to singular inventions in all of these fields. Among these responses is *reading*. It is only through the accumulation of individual acts of reading and responding, in fact, that large cultural shifts occur, as the inventiveness of a particular work is registered by more and more participants in a particular field.

Reading (and I include here listening to an utterance or mentally rehearsing a work known by heart) involves a number of different types of activity occurring simultaneously and not always in accord with one another. For purposes of analysis, we may isolate from these a basic reading procedure consisting of the mechanical conversion of typographic marks or phonetic sequences into conceptual structures, following the conventions of lexicography, syntax, genre, implicature, relevance, and so on. At the same time as it tries to decode the textual string with the necessary objectivity and accuracy, however, reading —and I am referring here to the reading of all kinds of text, not only those traditionally classified as literary—can be an attempt to respond to the otherness, inventiveness, and singularity of the work (three properties which, as we have seen, are closely inter-implicated). When it succeeds in apprehending otherness, in registering the singularity and inventiveness of the work, we may call a reading creative, by analogy with the other types of creativity noted earlier.[1]

This is not to say that there are two distinct modes of reading; rather that the always dominant mode of mechanical reading can be modified or interrupted by a somewhat different relation to the work. Not all works will have something to offer to a reader's openness to alterity, of course, but when one does, mechanical and instrumental interpretation is complicated by what we may term readerly hospitality, a readiness to have one's purposes reshaped by the work to which one is responding. The work in question may be a philosophical argument, an autobiography, a poem, or any number of other types of text: in every case, its inventiveness, otherness, and singularity cannot be apprehended by means of the application of existing norms, or even by an extension of those norms. (By contrast, its originality, as a historical fact about it, can be appreciated in this way.)

A creative reading is not one that overrides the work's conventionally determined meanings in the name of imaginative freedom but rather one that, in its striving to do full justice to the work, is obliged to go beyond existing conventions. It is a reading that is not entirely programmed by the work and the context in which it is read, including the psychological character of the reader, even though it is a response to (not simply a result of or reaction to) text and context—and in this sense it might be called a necessarily unfaithful reading. (Later in this chapter we shall take up the question of the difference between the creative reading of literature and that of other kinds of work.)

Reading creatively in this way may be described in terms similar to those I have used in describing other modes of creation, including creative responsiveness to another person. To read creatively in an attempt to respond fully and responsibly to the alterity and singularity of the text is to work against the mind's tendency to assimilate the other to the same, attending to that which can barely be heard, registering what is unique about the shaping of language, thought, and feeling in this particular work. It involves a suspension of habits, a willingness to rethink old positions in order to apprehend the work's inaugural power. (It is this rethinking that will continue to have effects as one reads other works.) In its encounter with the other, an encounter in which existing modes of thought and evaluation falter, creative reading allows the work to take the mind (understood in the broadest sense) to the borders of its accustomed terrain. And there is no single "correct" reading, just as there is no single "correct" way for an artist, in creating a new work, to respond to the world in which he or she lives.

All reading is an event as much as it is an act—we feel pulled along by the work as we push ourselves through it, and we do not simply *choose* to read in a certain way—but the event of creative reading is marked by the experience of alterity that, as we have found, is extremely difficult to articulate. It requires a peculiar kind of passivity that does not preclude a high degree of alertness—what Wordsworth meant by "wise passiveness," perhaps. And because reading happens as an event, there is no possibility of legislating in advance, as many critical theories have attempted to do, what is and is not relevant to a full response. We may want to exclude as illegitimate the author's intentions, or facts of his or her biography, or our own beliefs as readers, or the quality of the paper on which the text is printed, but the reality is that any of these factors, and dozens more, may enter into a reading that does justice to the alterity and singularity of the work.

Since the subjective refashioning that the work calls for is different for every subject, indeed for every reading, singularity, too, is in play from the start. To respond to the singularity of the work I read is thus to *affirm* its singularity in my own singular response, open not just to the signifying potential of the words on the page but also to the specific time and place within which the reading occurs, the ungeneralizable relation between this work and this reader.[2] A word often used in literary commentary is "sympathy," and while there is a danger that a term like this may seem to imply a simple matching between mind and work, it helpfully captures something of the positive openness that characterizes a fully responsive reading.

As I have already stressed, a created entity is not a simple material object but is constituted by norms or codes that, however new, can be at least partially deduced and duplicated, as well as inventively reformulated. Were this not the case, the object would simply remain opaque and uninterpretable. However, although no creation occurs without the operation of generalizable norms, it is only retrospectively that we can extract them as norms (and thus objectify the transition from the other to the same), and even this hypostatization remains revisable. An important part of a full response to a work that strikes me with the force of the new (and we should remember that this may be a work written centuries ago, or one I have read many times before) is thus an attempt to fathom its *modus operandi*, to achieve an accurate understanding of the repeatable rules according to which the work operates as a meaningful entity.[3]

If I succeed in fully specifying those rules, making it possible for me to imitate the work exactly, I will have converted it wholly from the other to the same; we can observe this happening at a cultural level when a work operates as a new formula for other works to follow but retains little inventiveness itself for later readers. In Chapter 3 we considered Surrey's invention of poulter's measure as a possible example of such total accommodation. To offer a reading, in the sense of a response that attempts to do justice to a work's singularity, is therefore both to explain what can be explained and to find a way of showing that even the fullest explanation does not exhaust the work's inventiveness, that this type of reading necessarily fails. The more convincing the explanation of the work, the more strongly its inexplicability and inexhaustibility as a work of literature emerge, and the more its singularity is affirmed.[4]

Another way of approaching the contrast between mechanical and creative reading is by considering the implications of the non-monolithic character of culture. There is no such thing as "a culture" in the sense of a homogeneous entity with clear and fixed boundaries; there are cultural assumptions, habits, practices, and products that can be grouped in constellations, but the groupings are internally disparate and flow into one another, can be divided into smaller groups or amalgamated into larger ones, and are subject to continual change. Each of us inhabits what I have been calling an idioculture, the deposit of our personal history as a participant in a number of ill-defined and often conflicting cultural fields, overlapping with or nested within one another. Any text we read—like any person we encounter—is the product of a unique cultural formation of this kind; the process of reading, therefore, is the process of subjecting the assumptions of the cultural fields that make up my own distinctive idioculture to those which the work embodies (not, of course, as the simple reflex of its time but as it is read in my own time). And the more fully I have absorbed the cultural materials that surround me—including those that make up the institution of literature (its history, its range, its linguistic and generic conventions)—the richer the encounter is likely to be.

In a response that is necessarily unique—for no other reader or reading could be constituted within the same cultural matrix—I will usually find both familiarity and alterity, both recognition and strangeness. But for a number of reasons this can never be a simple or repeatable procedure: both the work's and my cultural fields are internally incoherent, some parts of the work's cultural fields may be inaccessible to me, and my own idioculture is in a permanent condition of change. Just as creation, the welcoming of the other, can occur only because the culture in which it occurs is constituted by exclusions and tensions, so creative reading can occur only because the reader's idioculture is fractured and pressured and thus open to alterity. To invert the statement with which the previous chapter ended, in a creative reading it is only as a singularity that I can respond to the singularity of the work.

Surprise and wonder

Creative reading, like any full response to alterity, is, as I have continually stressed, both active and passive. Focusing on the active aspect, I have talked of making an effort to do justice to the singularity of the other and to suspend habitual modes of thinking and feeling in order to be able to do this. Some kind of preparedness is necessary; without it, the work will be processed in terms of familiar norms and predispositions and received merely as a further example of the same. Yet it is also the case that to experience alterity as alterity, to register the singularity of the inventive work (like the singularity of the other person), is to be surprised by it, just as the inventor is surprised by the invention. There is no prescription that can be followed to ensure that alterity will emerge, no guarantee that a particular mode of reading will result in an experience of a work's inventiveness and singularity.

We cannot insist on logic, or chronology, here: I can welcome a work as other only if I have prepared for this possibility, and yet the event I have prepared for will occur only if it exceeds all my preparations and takes me unawares. In a passage in *The Master of Petersburg*, Coetzee's hero faces up to this failure of logic, as he acknowledges that the true surprise is one that cannot be foreseen, even as an anticipated surprise:

> If he expects his son to come as a thief in the night, and listens only for the call of the thief, he will never see him. If he expects his son to speak in the voice of the unexpected, he will never hear him. As long as he expects what he does not expect, what he does not expect will not come. Therefore—paradox within paradox, darkness swaddled in darkness—he must answer to what he does not expect. (80)

Levinas's quarrel with the dominant tradition of Western philosophy and the educational methods it has spawned arises from his perception that they are dedicated to the mastery of otherness, leaving no room for surprise; whereas for him, true philosophical understanding, and true teaching and learning, can be achieved only in being surprised by the other. The difficulty which he never entirely overcomes, though it is the focus of much of his writing, lies in spelling out how it is that the subject can achieve an openness to surprise.

"Surprise" is itself, though a useful word in this context, not without problems. It denotes, here, the experience of a reordering of habitual modes of thought and emotion, an experience which arises from an encounter with an entity, an idea, a form, a feeling that cannot be accounted for, cannot even be registered, by those habitual modes. To be surprised by the work is already to have responded to it, before any conscious effort at understanding. But notwithstanding the usual connotations of the word, it need not happen suddenly or as a single event: it is more likely to be gradual, fitful, mixed with many other responses. (We observed something very similar in relation to the process of invention.) If I say *The Decline and Fall of the Roman Empire* surprised me, I am probably not referring to a specific moment in my reading of Gibbon's massive history, but rather to one element in my protracted endeavor of coming to terms with the work—the historical arguments, the distinctive style, or some other feature or features. My first encounter with a work may make very little impact upon me at all: it may come across as nonsense, if it is in a completely unfamiliar mode (Mallarmé's "Un coup de dés," say, or Walter Abish's *Alphabetical Africa*), or as a mere repetition of a kind of writing with which I am all too familiar (Drayton's sonnets, perhaps, or Trollope's novels). Only with further readings, attentive to the work's singular fusion of generic and linguistic materials, does it register sufficiently as a literary work that blends familiarity and surprise.

There is a strong connection between surprise and *wonder*, and the latter word forms a useful complement to the former in our attempt to specify the singularity of a creative response to artworks, suggesting as it does a kind of lasting surprise—a paradox that is a feature of artistic invention. (Aristotle's term *thaumazein*, for him an important element in aesthetic pleasure, can in fact mean both surprise and wonder.[5]) Wonder is most closely associated with the tradition of the sublime in art and in nature (it is used by Longinus, for example), but can be regarded as an ingredient in a full response to the inventiveness of any work of art. It follows from my earlier argument that what we wonder at in such a response is, in every sense, the *invention*: that which was invented and is now before us, the inferred act-event by means of which it was invented, and the inventiveness of the creator or creators which was, and remains, revealed therein. In the literary field, one component of the wonder inspired by the work is a sense of the power of words: how extraordinary that the language we use every day can be made to function with this precision, or this forcefulness, or this grace! Notwithstanding the long tradition of connecting art and nature when discussing sublimity, wonder as an aspect of creative reading is therefore quite distinct from wonder at natural objects.

A further point that must be stressed is that—though this may itself seem a surprising thing to say—the reader does not always recognize that an event of creative reading is taking place. My use of the word "surprise," together with my frequent use of the word "experience," is potentially misleading, as though reading creatively were to be understood entirely in psychological terms, something we register consciously as a mental and perhaps emotional sequence. Of course, as I have stressed, there is usually a psychological dimension to an encounter with alterity (though it may take a host of different forms), but the event itself is not necessarily one of which the subject is wholly aware.[6] It may be a long time before the changes wrought by such an encounter make themselves felt—indeed, they may never reach consciousness. There is also the possibility that a work may be held in memory for a lengthy period without its potential for surprise being activated, before some other event triggers a new and creative engagement with it (just as there may be a delay before an inventive work has an effect on a culture).

It is worth stressing that the mere fact of a text's changing the subject who reads it does not signal an inventive work and a creative reading. To take an obvious example, the advertising industry relies on the power of certain kinds of texts to change the behavior of readers. Advertisements often rely on surprise to achieve their effects, but they seldom involve the kind of inventiveness and singularity I have been discussing; that is, they seldom invite creative readings that will introduce into the culture the hitherto unthinkable. They are much more likely to reinforce existing tendencies in the culture, and if they challenge existing habits and expectations it is in order to encourage other habits and expectations that will be more profitable for the advertiser. Although there are occasional exceptions, advertising, like some of what is classed as literature, cannot as a general rule risk the unpredictability of hospitality toward the other.

Surprise need not be opposed to the experience of recognition or intimacy discussed in the previous chapter: I can be surprised by the closeness of a work to me, the way it seems to echo what I had assumed to be my private thoughts, the fact that I experience familiarity where I expected to find only strangeness. We may feel that a work we are reading speaks directly to our deepest selves, yet when we look back we have to acknowledge that we had no awareness of those aspects of our subjectivity before the reading that offered itself as an affirmation of them. To apprehend the other is to acknowledge both an outer and an inner potentiality, while rendering that very distinction suspect.

Literary reading

So far in this chapter, I have been discussing the creative reading of a singular work without attempting to distinguish between the literary and the non-literary. But we may draw on our earlier discussions of the distinctiveness of literary invention and singularity to delineate the characteristics of literary reading. If I read a philosophical work creatively as philosophy, what I am responding to is the inventiveness, alterity, and singularity of the arguments and ideas embodied in language (and perhaps other sign systems); the same would be true of a work of economics, mathematics, or chemistry. A historical work or an autobiography may be read creatively as the representation of persons, events, and objects, inventively described and related to one another. The importance of John Rawls's *Theory of Justice* or Benedict Anderson's *Imagined Communities*, for example, lies in the number of inventive readings—in both senses—these books have received, issuing in influential teaching, further publications, and political action. To the extent, however, that I am responding to the words in which these arguments and representations are couched, in their singular and inventive arrangement, my creative reading partakes of the literary.

To respond fully to a work that presents itself as literary one has to be embedded in the culture of which literature, and perhaps this literary form, is a part, and one has to deploy one's familiarity with the conventionalized routines of the literary institution. A great deal of patient labor is unavoidable if a responsible reading is to be achieved; but it represents only the foundation of such a reading.[7] It brings the work into the orbit of the same; it treats it as an object whose configurations can be objectively studied and reported on.

The more fully this procedure is carried out on a work, the more clearly a unique object stands out, different from every other work. (We saw the beginnings of such a procedure in discussing Blake's "Sick Rose" in Chapter 5.) However, its uniqueness in this sense consists solely in a particular configuration of a large number of coded elements—word-meanings, grammatical categories, dates, places, reported events, allusions to other works, rhythmic features, and echoes of sound, to name only a few. It remains fully within the same; it makes no demand on habitual frameworks; it requires no judgment. The same type of analysis could in principle be carried out on any text of any kind, and it would emerge as unique, just as each snowflake is said to be unique. When a reading of a work is *literary*, it is more than a response to its particular collocation of coded elements; it is a response to a singularity that cannot be analyzed, yet remains recognizable across all repetitions of reading.

My depiction of the act of reading a literary work is still misleading in one important respect: I have been talking as if the work were a pre-existing object to which the reader, wholly independent of it, responds, whereas it is in fact a set of coded signals which become a poem or a novel only in a specific reading, and within which the reader too comes into being (as a singular subject partly produced in the reading of the work). Reading a work therefore makes it happen, "enacts" it in a way which is ambiguous—like the word "act"—as to its initiatory and mimetic functions. More specifically, a reading is a performance of the singularity and otherness of the writing that constitutes the work as it comes into being for a particular reader in a particular context. We shall return to the question of response later in this chapter and the question of performance in Chapter 7.

Re-reading

In his sonnet "On Sitting Down to Read *King Lear* Once Again," Keats bids farewell to "golden-tongued Romance" and turns to a different mode of reading:

> Adieu! for, once again, the fierce dispute
> Betwixt damnation and impassion'd clay
> Must I burn through; once more humbly assay
> The bitter-sweet of this Shakespearian fruit.

The account I have given of the literary event may seem to allow for no explanation of the phenomenon Keats is addressing: that the repetition of a reading experience can be as powerful as, or even more powerful than, the initial reading experience. We are all familiar with the feeling of enriched understanding and heightened intensity in re-reading a work, and we have probably all said after finishing a particularly inventive work of literature: "I need to read that again." One aspect of this phenomenon is, of course, that a work being re-read is very different from a work being read for the first time: the knowledge of what is to come in a work one has read before and the memory of the experience of earlier readings transform the reader's experience. However, re-reading can continue to offer fresh rewards well beyond a second or third occasion, when one might expect these factors to be relatively insignificant.

How this happens can be understood by returning to our discussion of a culture's response to an inventive work or *oeuvre*, both in its time and later. Just as a body of work can change expectations to the degree that it begins to be less inventive in relation to its audience (Wordsworth's "I wandered lonely as a cloud" has never been as inventive as when it first appeared), so a work that has a strong effect the first time it is read can have a reduced impact thereafter. But the reverse is often the case. However familiar the work is to me (and familiarity is, of course, part of the pleasure of much re-reading, though it is a peculiarly literary pleasure), it can always strike me with the force of novelty if, by means of a creative reading that strives to respond fully to the singularity of the work in a new time and place, I open myself to its potential challenge. Exact repetition never occurs, since the reader, and the cultural context in which and by means of which the reading takes place, constantly change. Every reading of a literary work that does justice to its singularity is itself an irreducibly singular event.

This explains the phenomenon of repeated suspense: knowing how a fictional narrative ends need not diminish the experience of increasing tension during the reading. Far from being the result of complete immersion in the events being related, so that we forget we are in a fictional world and respond as if to reality, this characteristic of literature springs from the fact that we remain well aware of the fabricated (and authored) nature of what we read. The suspense that is created, when it is literary suspense and not simply a response to events represented in language, does not depend on ignorance of what will happen but on the process of tension-making that the reader is taken through in full cognizance of what is happening. Suspense is staged, performed for and by the reader, whether it is the first or fifteenth encounter with the work. It is much harder for the historian to create suspense when the outcome of the events being described is well known; indeed, he or she is very likely to use literary devices to achieve this end.

The inventiveness of a literary work can, in part, be measured by its capacity to be re-read without loss of power; an uninventive work simply confirms my predispositions and expectations each time I read it. The effect of re-reading also offers a way of distinguishing between literary and non-literary works. In responding to the inventiveness of a non-literary work (or the non-literary inventiveness of a work that is also literary), there is no point in returning once I have registered the point of its new formulations. Re-reading the work simply repeats the process, and is only worth doing if I fail to grasp the work's argument, or I forget what I had gleaned the first time round. Re-reading the literary work, by contrast, is an affirmation of its literariness.

Reading as response

There is nothing new in the idea that a reading of a work of literature is a response to its uniqueness. Among literary criticism's watchwords have been for many decades the cluster "respond," "response," "responsiveness": students of literature in the most traditional classrooms are taught, usually via the medium of other people's responses, to respond fully and sensitively—that is, with appropriate responsiveness—to literary works. We might think of I. A. Richards's influential campaign against "stock responses": pre-formed views and emotions associated with particular phenomena, triggered by certain words and phrases and thus inhibiting full engagement with the work.[8] A list of all the adjectives used with "response" as laudatory in this context would bring out the range of the term's applications; they include "full," "adequate," "accurate," "appropriate," "true," "legitimate," "fitting," "just," "apt."

The notions of response and responsiveness are, however, more problematic than has usually been acknowledged. When, in a pedagogic mode derived from New Criticism (and which is still the norm in high schools and probably in undergraduate classes as well), students are taught to respond sensitively and fully to a literary work, they are expected to detect the unique and permanent significance of the work in question (or what the teacher, representing a cultural tradition, takes this significance to be). At the same time, there is also an insistence on responsiveness as a mark of the individual *reader's* unique identity; students of literature are encouraged to develop their "own" responses, and censured if they merely reduplicate someone else's response. A student handing in an essay that largely repeated an existing critical work would not expect high praise, no matter how accurately it represented what was held to be the work's essence.

These two demands are obviously in conflict, but both are imperative: to relax one would be to encourage willful subjectivism, to relax the other would foster mechanical plagiarism. To create an answering work that is itself unique is, it seems, the most adequate way of responding to the uniqueness of the work being read. That the most widespread classroom practice in literary studies is built upon a paradox is not a mark against it (though it can be censured for its failure to acknowledge and account for the paradox); rather, it is an indication of the complexity of the notion of response. How does the response relate to the work it follows? It must, clearly, be different from it: a response is not an echo or a reflection; it has no value if it is entirely programmed by the text. And yet to *be* a response and not an arbitrary event that happens to come after the work it must in some way repeat the work. Furthermore, what it must repeat in its avoidance of repetition is not just any element of the work, but the very thing that makes it unique—otherwise it will not be a response to that particular work, and hence not a response at all, merely a reaction.

It is not a matter of an act calling forth a wholly secondary and subsidiary reaction, then, but of a *reenactment* that, paradoxically, makes the "original" act happen, and happen differently with each such response. What is more, the text as text, as unique literary work, achieves its full existence only in my reading of it, and what I am calling "my response" is to something that is constituted in that response. Just as my response to another person as other is a response to the other in its relating to me, so my response to a work is not to the work "itself" but to the work as other in *the event of its coming into being in my reading*. As with many other nouns in this book, a clumsier but strictly preferable term would be "responding," as there is no entity and no closure involved, only a repeatable, though always different, happening.

We can now reinterpret the impossible demand for a response that is both faithful and original. The uniqueness to which the response must do justice is not an unchanging essence, nor the sum of the work's difference from all other works as it appears in a particular time and place, but the inventive otherness of the work as it emerges through my creative act of comprehension (and my acknowledgment of its limits), that is to say, its *singularity*. The only way I can affirm and sustain the singularity of the work is by a singular response, since my response grows out of the particular act of reading. It will be a response that takes account of all the programmable procedures that the institution of literature requires in a full account of its formal arrangements of meaning and referentiality (and to this degree it will be part of the general practice of criticism). But my response will also be an unpredictable, singular affirmation of the singular event of the work's otherness as it impinges on me, here and now, in this event of reading. (We may recall Kant's distinction between "imitating" and "following" a work of genius—see Chapter 3 above.) I will be responding not only as a cultural representative but as a singularity not exhausted by my culture's determinations. And since what I respond to creatively is brought into being by my response, there can be no simple separation or chronology here: a creative reading displaces the opposition of inside and outside, before and after. It can do this only as an event which is also the experience of an event.

Literary works themselves have been among the most notable examples of the creative response to singularity—sometimes in the guise of imitations, translations, or extrapolations (examples might include Pound's *Homage to Sextus Propertius*, Stoppard's *Rosencrantz and*

Guildenstern Are Dead, Coetzee's *Foe* and *The Master of Petersburg*), and always with the "unfaithfulness" of which I have spoken. All good translations operate in this manner, too. What is more, there is no possibility of classifying critical responses into "creative" or "mechanical" with any kind of objectivity or finality: a creative response to a literary work can be identified only in a further response to *its* singularity—only, that is, when it functions inventively.

Reading as invention

A creative reading often moves to an articulation in words, as if the work being read demanded a new work in response.[9] Coetzee explains his need to write about Kafka as follows:

> My experience is that it is not reading that takes me into the last twist of the burrow, but writing. No intensity of reading that I can imagine would succeed in guiding me through Kafka's word-labyrinth: to do that I would once again have to take up the pen and, step by step, write my way after him. (*Doubling the Point*, 199)

A verbal articulation of this kind—in a conversation, an article, a lecture, a letter—may itself function inventively to make possible, through singular responses by other readers, new ways of writing, new ways of reading. An inventive reading (and now "reading" takes on its meaning of "commentary") is, of course, subject to all the conditions under which invention functions, including both the necessity of close engagement with the cultural context and the effects of historical shifts.

In fact, this process—the inventive work giving rise to the inventive response—is how *all* invention occurs. For invention is never a matter of creation *ex nihilo*; it is always, as I have been arguing throughout this book, a response. Putting it generally, it is a response to a cultural situation in which the pressures and fractures inherited from the past make possible the emergence of what has been suppressed or disguised; but this cultural situation is manifested in particular inventive works (we are talking for the moment of all kinds of cultural products), and it is in response to these works that fresh inventions arise. The inventive literary writer may not be aware of all (or indeed any) of the works to which he or she is responding, but this is not to be wondered at: we have already noted how little the inventor may understand of the process of invention.

In an inventive response the reader attempts to answer to the work's shaping of language by a new shaping of his or her own (which will in turn invite further responses)—whether it be in the form of a literal act of writing, an inward composition, a speech or intervention in a discussion, a change of behavior. What this means, of course, is that it in turn will partake of the literary to some degree, and demand of its readers a response of the same inventive kind. This prospect of an endless chain of responses may sound alarming, but it only becomes so if we conceive of literature as possessing an extractable content which can finally be isolated—and hence possessing those qualities of self-presence, universality, historical transcendence, and absolute signification on which the Platonic tradition of aesthetics is based. But literature is characterized precisely by its lack of any such content—which, of course, is why we re-read, with no end in sight of our re-readings.

Performance 7

Literary performance

We have seen that the linguistic event can function inventively in two different ways: in the non-literary work, where its results are what matter, and in the literary work, where the *eventness* of the event is what matters—although we must not forget that a single work can function in both these ways, even in a single reading. In the second case the reader experiences not just the event itself, but its happening *as event*. Another way of putting this is that the literary work exists only in *performance*.[1]

I choose the term "performance" to designate creative literary reading partly because it usefully points to a feature which we have not yet considered and which is often overlooked: an element of self-distance present in the event of the literary, the linguistic event comprehended in its eventness. (Once more, were it not for its awkwardness, I might prefer the term "performing," which avoids any implication that we are dealing with an entity rather than an event.) Most of the sentences we read or hear we do not perform, in this sense; we recognize, apprehend, interpret them, perhaps feel or do something as an immediate consequence, but we treat their words cognitively and instrumentally.

Take the referential properties of a text: I may enjoy and learn from my encounter with the concepts, feelings, historical or imagined entities, and so on, to be found in any text, including a literary text (which always functions in ways other than the literary). But when, in conjunction with other modalities of reading, I respond to a text *as literature* (and it may or may not impose this choice upon me), my pleasure and profit come from the experience of an event of referring, from a staging of referentiality, not from any knowledge I acquire.[2]

Fiction is not, therefore, identical with literature; a fictional work may simply present fictional characters and events for my delectation, as in an anecdote or perhaps—this would have to be argued case by case and would always be subject to revision—certain novels that lack inventiveness at any level. More accurately, fiction and literature refer to different modes of reading: I can read *Middlemarch* as fiction without at the same time reading it as literature. (It is unlikely, however, that I would be able to read it as literature without reading it as fiction.) Literary fiction involves the *performance* of fictionality, occurring as the experience of an event or a series of events whereby the characters and occurrences apparently being referred to are in fact, and without this fact being disguised, brought into being by the language.

To take another mode of signification that has played a central part in the literary tradition and in accounts of the literary: allegory, the device whereby the meanings of a work are understood as themselves signifying further, and ultimately more important, meanings. Allegory, or the possibility of allegorical reading, is not itself a defining property of the literary—it is, for instance, common in religious discourse; but the performance of "allegoricity," the pleasure taken in the event of allegorizing, is a literary phenomenon.[3] The biblical Song of Solomon can be read both as a doctrinal text conveying an understanding of the individual's or the Church's relation to the godhead and as a literary work which stages the undecidability between carnal and spiritual love—and it can be read in both these ways at once.

Similarly, narrative becomes literary when it involves the performance of narrativity, metaphor when it involves the performance of metaphoricity, mimesis when it involves the performance of mimetivity, description when it involves the performance of descriptivity, and so on. (Even these nouns—some of them invented for the purpose—are somewhat misleading, as our response is not to an attribute or a substance, but to an event: more clumsily, we could speak of the performing of narrating, metaphorizing, imitating, describing.) We enjoy narrative, metaphor, and description in all kinds of texts without thereby responding to them as literary; only in a literary response to a work that calls for such a response do we enjoy them for showing simultaneously what they are and what they can do.

Thus the tradition of realist fiction should be understood—in so far as it is literature and not a type of history read for its vivid representation of past events—as a staging of objectivity, an invitation to experience the knowability of the world. We learn from literature not truth, but what the telling (or denying) of the truth is. Recent criticism has often stressed the power of literary works as witnesses to historical traumas; here again, the works in question function in several ways at once, and there is no contradiction involved in saying that, as testimonies, they witness in a powerful manner and at the same time, as literary works, they stage the activity of witnessing. (This staging produces a pleasurable intensity which will often make the literary work more effective as a witness than a historical work.) Other literary works offer the contrary experience of the unknowability of the world, or of elements in it: other people, the past, the future, oneself.

More generally, literature does not present themes as such, but rather takes the reader through a process of thematizing. We can of course summarize the theme of this or that poem or play, but we are usually conscious that in doing so we have omitted everything that makes the work a literary artifact. Even Aristotle's somewhat surprising insistence that the tragic emotions may be aroused merely by hearing the plot of a play such as *Oedipus Rex* implies a performance (in speech) of the events in their proper order, rather than a statement of its themes. This may also be the place to raise the question of beauty—set aside in the introduction—once more: whereas we may experience beauty in a number of entities, natural or humanly constructed, the artwork enables us to live through the process of beauty-making, of the becoming-beautiful—and sometimes the ceasing-to-be-beautiful. Similarly, literary works frequently invite us to make moral judgments, but to move from the staging of judgment to the judgments themselves is to move beyond the literary.

What of a work that is presented to an audience as a performance, whether a simple recitation of a poem by a reader (including the poet him- or herself), or a full-scale theatrical production? There is much more to be said about this issue than I can deal with here, but the point to be stressed is that the account I have given of reading as performance applies equally to the events of listening to and watching the performances of others. True, there are great differences between performing a poem or a novel or the text of a play by reading it and "performing" the same work by hearing it read or seeing it presented on stage; but we must not be misled by these differences into thinking that the second category is a more passive one, in which the responsibility for performance is handed over lock, stock, and barrel to someone else. If I am responding creatively to a work being performed before me, if I am doing justice to its singularity, alterity, and inventiveness, I am still active in performing it—which is also to say I am caught up in, and partly constituted as a subject by, the event of performance.

There is an important distinction to be made between the two modes of literary performance, however. Take a play that is being performed before me: if I am responding creatively to it, I am performing not just "the play" but this performance of it. As I perform the performance, I respond not only to the potential written into the work by the author or authors but also to the work of the artists involved in making the performance happen—the director, actors, designers, and so on.[4] Responding to a poem being recited involves performing the particular performance of it that I am hearing. It may even be the case that when I read a poem aloud myself I respond creatively to my own performance as a realization of the performative potential of the work.

A recent anthology of "close readings" announces on its back cover that the book presents "a wide range of responses to the question at the heart of literary criticism: how best to read a text to understand its meaning."[5] My argument is that a very different question should be at the heart of literary criticism and exemplified by the best close reading: how best to perform a text's engagements with linguistic power. For anything that language can do in the world may be performed in literature. In performing the work, I am taken through its performance of language's potency; indeed, I, or the "I" that is engaged with the work, could be said to be performed by it. This performed I is an I in process, undergoing the changes wrought by, and in, the encounter with alterity.

Literary performance: an example

Let us consider a brief example. Here is a stanza by George Herbert, from the poem "Easter":

> I got me flowers to straw thy way;
> I got me boughs off many a tree:

But thou wast up by break of day,
And brought'st thy sweets along with thee.[6]

To read or hear this as literature is to experience the singular event of its four lines, to be carried forward by a familiar, rather insistently regular rhythm, to register the easy colloquialism of the phrasing and the simplicity of the syntax, and to counterpoise against these experienced qualities the extraordinariness of the occurrence—the coming to life of a man who was lying dead in a tomb—to which it refers. As with "The Sick Rose," it is to participate in an ambiguous, perhaps even contradictory, tonal and emotional complex—reverence? whimsicality? awe? disappointment? delight? triumph? It is to feel, as one reads them, the anticipation built up by the first two lines—the second a variation on the first—and the sudden explosion of meaning in the third on the apparently insignificant word "up," where a trifling observation about rising from sleep expressed in the most flat and elementary phrasing—"thou wast up," you were up—refers to a barely imaginable occurrence, one that has taken place, as it were, in the space between the previous line and this one. It is to undergo the transition from this moment of shock to a final line, conveying its finality in meter and rhyme, of course, but also in the clinching and calming thought of the sweetness (physical and spiritual) accompanying the risen Christ, outstripping by an unthinkable distance all human efforts at solicitude and celebration. It is also, at the same time, *to be made aware of language's power to do all these things*, to be made conscious of their happening as a complex linguistic (but also, and inseparably, a conceptual, emotional, and physical) event. For a moment, the reader who undergoes all this experiences a miracle, and experiences it as a miracle in language.

A reading of the poem that activates such qualities is a performance of it, whether spoken aloud, heard in someone else's reading, read silently on the page, or recited in the mind from memory, and it is in such performances that it comes into being, each time, as a poem. Every performance is different from all others, sometimes in imperceptible ways (an example might be a single reader reading it for a second and then a third time in quick succession)[7] but often in marked ways (as would emerge if, for instance, we could compare a performance in the seventeenth century with one today). Reading the poem as a literary work is different from reading it for, say, the purposes of doctrinal instruction, or as historical evidence; these are not performances but interpretations geared to the extraction of truth. Performing the poem as a literary reader may involve being alert to doctrinal and historical issues—this may well be one of the criteria of a good reading of Herbert's work—but it also involves a certain suspension of questions of truth, of morality, of history. One need have no belief in the Resurrection to perform Herbert's poem and to feel the power of its literary eventness—though one does need to understand, and feel, what it is to believe.

My example can be no more than suggestive; as a singular work, whose singularity is renewed in each performance of it, its inventiveness differs from the inventiveness of every other singular work, and no simple extrapolation or generalization is possible. As I have been emphasizing, part of what an inventive work discovers, and makes possible for other writers, is new ways of being inventive. Nor, to reiterate another point made earlier, is my example intended to advance a new way of doing literary criticism; critics have often commented on literature (especially poetry) in terms that suggest the centrality of what I am calling inventiveness and singularity, and the way in which these properties are realized in performances of language's powers. A large body of criticism has, however, failed to distinguish between the performativity of the literary work and other, non-literary aspects of it, such as its referential accuracy, its moral stance, its political usefulness, its formal complexity, its narrative structure, and so on. As we have already noted, it has often been highly inventive writers who have responded most fully to other literary works, and this is hardly surprising: commentary on a work that seeks to do justice to its eventness must find a way of conveying that quality in a second work, and so it, too, must have a performative dimension.

Authoredness

There is another aspect of the performance of literature that needs to be taken into account, one that is sometimes given short shrift in current theoretical discussions of signification and interpretation. I have referred to the assumption held by the reader of a text (whether literary or not) as to the purposiveness of the sentences he or she is reading (p. 57 above). Whether the assumption is literally true or false, it underlies the experience of meaning in the reading of any text. This is not to say that meaning can be identified with authorial intention, although this is how many readers, if asked, would describe the experience, and from time to time attempts are made to translate this intuition into a theory of meaning-as-intention. The problems produced by such a conception of intention have been well aired in the past sixty years. What I want to suggest, rather, is that a precondition for meaningfulness of the sort characteristic of the verbal text is an assumption (conscious or unconscious) on the part of the reader of an intention to mean, or perhaps to resist or attenuate meaning, on the part of an author or authors. We are dealing only with a process of inference here: there is no possibility of a recourse to anything like an intention "itself." Even if we could gain access to the authorial mind we would not find anything like a simple intention. (However, many works, both literary and non-literary, create the illusion that we are gaining access to the author's intentions—what we might call the "intentionality effect."[8])

This underlying sense of purposiveness is manifested as what we may term "authoredness," the presupposition that the words we are reading are the product of a mental event or a number of such events whereby the processes of linguistic meaning are engaged.[9] We may know nothing about the author of a particular text, not even his or her name, but we read the text on the assumption that it is authored, that it is the work, however mediated, of at least one, almost certainly human, mind.[10] Authoredness arises not from communion with the creator but, like all aspects of the work's meaning, from the social and cultural context within which art is received. It is part of a wider process of historicization that runs through the way we interpret the made world (even if it often involves fantasy as much as factual reconstruction). Although the assumption of authoredness is highly characteristic of Western art, and probably has been since at least the Classical period of Greek culture, there is no reason to assume that in other cultures practices that look like what we know as "art"—dancing, story-telling, the fabrication of artifacts—carry any implication of authorial responsibility.

While authoredness is a necessary feature of all verbal meaning, the authoredness of a literary work is especially significant, because of the part played by invention in its production and reception. Invention is, as I have stressed, as much an event that happens to the inventor (and the culture) as an act arising out of a set of intentions, as much an occurrence in the domain of the community as in that of the individual. I have argued that we experience inventiveness as an otherness in the process of being translated into, while at the same time transforming, our inherited cultural norms and proclivities. Although we can say that this happens to us as it happened to the inventor, it does not happen as the same experience, but rather as a consequential one. Nevertheless, the sense of authoredness remains crucial: an invention is not wholly to be explained as a self-generated eruption in the cultural field, but has as its site of origin a mind or group of minds. We may experience a natural object—a leaf, a waterfall, a cloud—as singular and other, and its singularity and alterity may produce a reshaping of our habitual modes of apprehension in the manner that we have seen is the sign of alterity, but (if we can leave aside anthropomorphic theology) we do not experience it as an invention. In the previous chapter I observed that the wonder that forms part of a full response to an artwork is quite different from that which may be generated by a natural object precisely in that its source is the invention, in every sense, that is being experienced.

We have noted that the experience of the inventive literary work (usually, but not always, registered as a conscious and pleasurable opening of possibilities) arises not from the *content* of the invention, the series of arguments or the proposed concepts it puts forward, but from the reader's *performance* of it—and its performance of the reader. The sense of authoredness, therefore, relates very closely to the inventive production of the work. What I affirm when I respond to the text in a way that does justice to its otherness is not simply a particular argument or arrangement of words but what I take to be the creativity of its imputed author or authors in bringing into existence that argument or those words.[11] While many of our encounters with language, and perhaps the greater part of our experience of any linguistic text, written or spoken, operate without this assumption, a full response to the otherness of the literary work includes an awareness of, a respect for, and in a certain sense (to which I shall return in Chapter 9) a taking of responsibility for, the creativity of its author. This is not a matter of trying to reproduce the experience of writing innovatively which I attempted to sketch at the beginning of Chapter 2 (what I called "the creation of the other"); the processes of creation (which will probably have involved revision over time) have now been left behind.[12] Nor am

I responding to the originality of the work, which is a matter of historical reconstruction, as we saw in an earlier section.

Another way of putting this argument about authoredness is that to read a text in the fullest sense—in contrast to mechanically decoding it—is to treat it not as a static assemblage of words but as the "written," or even better—because it captures the unending activity involved—as *a writing*. There are texts that demand only decoding, texts that carry no implication of having been written. Take, for example, the proper name of the manufacturer I see stamped on my computer as I write: I am not likely to read this in any full sense, unless it displays a peculiar inventiveness or linguistic density. But most of what I read, I read as writing, which is to say as words which have in some sense been chosen and arranged. This choosing and arranging can, and of course very often does, lack any particular creativity. Where it is, or rather can in a creative reading be taken to be, creative—in the sense I have given the term—it seems appropriate to call the written object a *work*, suggesting as this word does the labor that went into its creation. In this it corresponds well with the double meaning of "invention." By contrast, "text" (as Roland Barthes liked to remind his readers) suggests an unauthored weave of linguistic signs, and seems more appropriate for the vast quantity of uncreative writing. (This is, of course, not the use Barthes made of the term.) We must not allow the resonances of the term "work" to echo too strongly, however; although we may admire the time and effort that has gone into an invention, what we respond to when we respond creatively and responsibly is the enduring event of invention that the labor made possible, not to the labor as such—to the work as working rather than as worked.

The temporality of the literary work

It is something of a truism that a literary work is a temporal event rather than a static object, but one that can point to two distinct properties of the work: as having its origin in a series of creative acts whose final product, though produced in time, gives an illusory appearance of stasis; or as emerging only in the act of a reading, which transforms the apparently static body of words on the page into a temporal performance. The former kind of temporality is most vividly illustrated in editions of texts that show stages of revision by means of graphic overlays (the synoptic edition of Joyce's *Ulysses* edited by Hans Walter Gabler is a well-known example); the latter is a commonplace in much practical criticism of poetry that treats the poem as a spoken event or dramatic scene and in much narrative theory in which sequentiality is a crucial element. The two conceptions of temporality tend to exclude one another: an emphasis on the fluid processes of creative choice and the multiplicity of alternative textual possibilities undermines the notion of a simply linear spoken performance, while commentary on the work as a speech or series of events unfolding in time tends to take as its script a single, completed, authorized text.

The challenge is to think both these temporalities together. The literary work does not come from nowhere, and a sense of its having been written in a temporal process is part of our understanding of it. (We can, as I have stressed, be fooled; there is no final guarantee that the work we read was in fact produced by intentional behavior in a human creative act—but the assumption that it was so produced inescapably colors our reading of it.) The question "What did the author mean by writing this?" is not a question that will go away, despite all our sophistication about fallacies of intentionalism—though it need not imply the availability of answers in some realm prior to the work. Historical and biographical research can suggestively enrich our sense of the writing process, as it occurred in a particular time and place, though it can never close down the text's movement toward openness. All this means that the temporality of creation, as a retrospectively constituted element in interpretation, is part of our understanding of any literary work. And yet the writtenness of the work remains unrealized until it is read, read in a singular enactment of its potential that puts into play many (but never all) of the possibilities encoded within it.

But there is more to the temporality of the literary work than these two dimensions. To call the work "a writing" rather than "the written," as I have suggested we might do, is to signal the curious temporality that governs our reading of literature. Even if the purpose of reading a work is to reconstruct a historical meaning, such as the sense that the work's first readers were likely to draw from it, the words as we read them produce their effects *in the present*. This present is unlike the present of the objects that I see around me, or of the words on the page as material entities; the very presentness of the words I read is premised on their pastness, on their having been written by another person in a different present.

The term "writing" used as a noun signals this paradoxical but familiar temporality: it implies that the activity of creating a text does not end when the author puts down the pen or exits the word-processing program. The text remains a writing as long as it is read. (If it is unread it is merely a "written.") In the conventions of commentary the interpenetration of past and present is signaled by the use of the present tense in literary criticism, whether in referring to the activity of writing—"The author here summarizes the argument"—or to the world brought into being by the text—"Fabrice is appalled by the guard's behavior." Nor is this only a critical habit: it is perfectly normal to say of a novel, "I loved the bit where he gets into the bath with his boots on." The undecidability between act and event that characterizes invention maps onto the temporal undecidability of reading writing: in so far as it is an act, reading responds to the *written*, performing interpretative procedures upon it (which include an awareness of the historical act carried out by an author); in so far as it is an event, reading is performed by the *writing*—indeed, it might be said that it is what the writing writes.

If, then, we say that the work is not an object or structure of signs possessing a meaning or set of meanings but an act that is also an event, an event that is also an act, we refer simultaneously to the act-event of writing and the act-event of reading. (Edward Said points out that in the best performances of music, the work seems to be presented "*as if* created by the performer"; and Antony Sher vividly describes the moment when the actor, in speaking a dramatic text, gets "a tiny sense of what it must've been like to write these words originally."[13]) The act of reading is clearly a response to the act of writing, but, as we saw above, the notion of "response" is a complex one, and the second act constitutes as well as follows from the first. In other words, although what I am calling the "act of writing" cannot be identified with the historical moment of composition, neither can it be divorced from that inventive moment.[14]

The literary work as other is the work in performance, a performance which estranges (without disempowering) all the fundamental operations of language. It is not constituted, that is, by an enduring nucleus but by the singular putting into play of—while also testing and transforming—the set of codes and conventions that make up the institution of literature and the wider cultural formation of which it is part. Its singularity, each time it is read, lies in its performance (in performing and being performed), and although, as we have seen, that singularity can only be apprehended as it turns into, and by virtue of, generality, it is reborn as a new singularity with each new performance.

Form, meaning, context 8

Form and the literary

In some kinds of text, the author's creative labor is centered on the manipulation of ideas, the construction of arguments, the representation of existing entities in a new light, or the imagination of hitherto non-existent entities. In other kinds of text, the ones we call literary, such labor is combined with, and is in a certain sense always subject to, the selection and arrangement of words. In these works, otherness and singularity arise from the encounter with the words themselves, their sequence, their suggestiveness, their patterning, their interrelations, their sounds and rhythms. To re-experience the otherness of a work of this type, it is not enough to recall the arguments made, the ideas introduced, the images conjured up; it is necessary to re-read or recall the words, in their created order. One way of saying this is that a creative achievement in the literary field is, whatever else it may be, a *formal* one.

The long history of the term "form" poses problems for anyone who wants to use it today. In literary studies it can refer to an abstract structure or arrangement ("the sonnet form") or the specific properties of a single work ("the unique form of Shakespeare's Sonnet 116"). (The German language usefully distinguishes between *Form* for the former and *Gestalt* for the latter.) Form is, as we saw in the first chapter of this book, associated with a static understanding of the art object, one in which content or meaning is opposed to the physical materials and their shape or structure. In literary criticism, form is usually contrasted with content but—notwithstanding the philosophical tradition descended from Plato and Aristotle—aligned with matter or substance: if you are interested in the phonic or graphic material of poetry, for instance, you are deemed a formalist. What we need is an account of form—or rather of some of the properties of writing that have given rise to the use of this term in literary criticism—that does not fall into the dualisms of the aesthetic tradition.

In particular, the opposition of form and content, which sets formal properties apart from any connection the work has to ethical, historical, and social issues, needs to be re-opened as a question. It is an opposition that remains implicit in the still-potent tradition of "organic form," which, while arguing for the possibility of a perfect fit between form and content that renders them inseparable, nevertheless relies on a prior theoretical separation. Most claims for the importance of form in literature operate on this model (including a large part of the discipline of stylistics, for example), and it is difficult to verbalize a positive response to the formal features of a work without using some version of the scheme whereby sound echoes sense, form enacts meaning. But unless we can rescue literary discourse from these oppositions, form will continue to be treated as something of an embarrassment to be encountered, and if possible evaded, on the way to a consideration of semantic, and thus historical, political, and ideological, concerns.[1]

The invention of the other whereby alterity is brought into the idiocultural, and beyond that the cultural, field cannot be thought of in terms of the separation of form and content. The new form that emerges, the new arrangement of cultural materials, is, by the same token, a new content—an open set of fresh possibilities of meaning, feeling, perceiving, responding, behaving. ("Meaning" and "feeling," like the other words in this list, should be understood as verbs, not nouns.) What we respond to in performing a literary work is evidently a complex involving both the formal and the semantic, but as long as we represent this complex as a static object, a representation which traditional notions of form tend to encourage, we are likely to fall into a simplified conception of it. If, however, we think of the work as an act-event, as a process that is essentially temporal taking place in the performance of a reader, it is possible to reconceptualize form and the literary work.

Formal inventiveness is not merely a matter of finding new ways of constructing sentences or managing verbal rhythms. The possibility of creating an otherness that has the effects I have been describing springs not just from the fact that words consist of certain sounds and shapes, but also from the fact that these sounds and shapes are nexuses of meaning and feeling, and hence deeply rooted in culture, history, and the varieties of human experience. The formal sequence therefore functions as a *staging* of meaning and feeling: a staging that is realized in what I have called a performative reading. Works of literature offer many kinds of pleasure, but one aspect of the pleasure that can be called peculiarly literary derives from this staging, this intense but distanced playing out of what might be the most intimate, the most strongly felt, constituents of our lives. Without the crucial functioning of form in the sense I have given it here, there would be no sense of staging, of a playing out in time. In the reading of the writing that is literature, one might say, meaning is simultaneously formed and performed. The words mean, and at the same time they show us what it is to mean.

Form and meaning

Instead of being opposed to content, then, form in the sense I am developing here includes the mobilization of meanings, or rather of the events of meaning: their sequentiality, interplay, and changing intensity, their patterns of expectation and satisfaction or tension and release, their precision or diffuseness. It does not include any extractable sense, information, image, or referent that the work lays before the reader. Through this mobilization of meanings, the work's linguistic operations such as referentiality, metaphoricity, intentionality, and ethicity are staged.

A necessary condition for a full response to the literary work therefore includes careful attention to, inter alia, the operation of reference, metaphor, intention, and ethics (prerequisites for the responsible reading of a text of any kind, as one relates it to its numerous contexts, past and present), since only through such attention can the work's staging of these relations be apprehended and shared. But this is not a sufficient condition: to go no further would be to treat the text as history, reportage, confession, sermon, or some other type of non-literary discourse. Only in working through the performance of these operations can one do justice to the work as a work of literature. Let me quickly add that this does not involve a reassertion of the traditional boundaries between literature and its textual others; on the contrary, it is to render those boundaries porous and problematic, since the "literariness" of any text is the degree to which (in a particular time and place) it is open to such a staging of the primary functions of language and discourse. I have already underscored the point that the distinction between works which do and do not rely upon a unique selection and arrangement of words for their inventiveness, singularity, and otherness does not correspond exactly to the culturally accepted (though historically mutable) categorization of texts as literary or non-literary. Many that are conventionally considered non-literary are characterized by formal creativity (and this aspect of their make-up may achieve longer-lasting recognition than their arguments or representations), whereas many texts we label as novels, poems, and plays are other only to the extent that they bring into existence powerful images or innovatively handle concepts. It is as an identification of the "literary" in *any* text that the focus on formal singularity and otherness (which, as we have seen, are not separable properties) is particularly useful.

The analogy of the signature which I have already used in connection with the recognizability of singular *oeuvres*—and which I borrow from Derrida[2]—may help to clarify this notion of form. A valid signature always carries the meaning: "I, the bearer of such-and-such a proper name, wrote this in person in a particular place and at a particular time, intending it as an act of authentication." In the act of reading and verifying the signature we need not be aware of the place and time (though often this is specified as well), but we must be aware of the situatedness and datedness—in one sense of the term—of the act of writing. To be able to verify that the signature is indeed a signature, however, and not just a proper name (inscribed by the bearer), the reader needs to be able to recognize it, either by an act of memory or by the act of physically checking it against other instances. Without such an act, it remains merely an inscribed name. The being of the signature, then, lies in the double act of writing and reading, not in the empirical object. (A signature produced by a mechanical stamp functions only as a representation of a signature, and works quite differently.) And the response to the signature as a signature—that is, to the singular act of writing of which it is the trace—is part of what constitutes it as a signature.[3]

In much the same way, the literary work is fully constituted as literary only in a response to it which confirms its literariness—which is to say, its existence as an act of writing dated from a time and place. (This sense of dating is one aspect of what I have called the experience of "authoredness," of "reading writing.") But what signals that it is literature? If we turn to the signature, we find that it is nothing but form; the traced record of an act of producing a certain visible shape in space.[4] Clearly, the literary work involves a great deal more than form, but it is as a written form—which is to say as the encrypted image of an act-event of invention, waiting to be re-enacted in a reading—that it identifies itself as literature, and as this unique (but always recognizable) work of literature. Not form as empirical structure, however, but form as performed mobility, as a performance of reading answering to a performance of writing. Unlike the literal signature, the literary work does not imply a single, located, dated act of writing, but it does have the general qualities of singularity, location, and datedness—by contrast with other types of writing which depend on an escape from these circumstances in order to fulfill their task of conveying meanings.[5]

Just as the operation of the signature depends on its formal uniqueness, the literary work derives its singularity from the formal act-event that constitutes it, and that is reconstituted in reading. However, the operation of the signature also relies on its being different on every occasion; as we have seen, mechanical reproduction will not suffice. It possesses the paradoxical quality of a singularity that is confirmed only in repetitions, and in repetitions that are different every time. Indeed, its singularity the "first" time (but when is the first time of a signature?) is already a product of generalities and differences—the differential codes that make for recognizable alphabetic writing. The literary work, too, continues to be repeated as the "same" event as long as it is read (that is, read as a literary work); but no reading is identical with any other one. Responding to the work as literary means responding to the singularity of its meaningful, affective movement, occurring in the renewable act of my performance; what it does not mean is carrying away from the text some conceptual substance for my further use or entertainment.

The performance of form: an example

Do not fear Baas.
It's just that I appeared
And our faces met
In this black night that's like me.

Do not fear—
We will always meet
When you do not expect me.
I will appear,
In the night that's black like me.
Do not fear—
Blame your heart
When you fear me—
I will blame my mind
When I fear you
In the night that's black like me.
Do not fear Baas,
My heart is vast as the sea
And your mind as the earth.
It's awright baas,
Do not fear.

The primary otherness of Mongane Wally Serote's poem, "The actual Dialogue,"[6] like that of any poem which can be said to open onto alterity, lies in its resistance to immediate assimilation and interpretation, its refusal to yield wholly to the codes and strategies we, as literary readers, are trained to bring to bear upon language and upon its ethical, aesthetic, constative, and performative uses—while at the same time it exists only by virtue of those codes and strategies. The power of Serote's poem, registered in the intellectual and emotional mutations required to absorb and comprehend it (to the degree that this is achievable), is a product of just these words; as I read the poem I have no thought that there might be more words added, or some changed or taken away. To re-experience (though never in quite the same way) the emotional/physical/intellectual complex that constitutes my response to the poem, and thus constitutes the poem, I need to re-experience these words, unaltered, in the same order.

This is what I take to be the fundamental point of using the term "form" to describe an individual literary work, and it will be clear that the notion of singularity is entirely bound up with the notion of form in this sense. What I carry away from my reading of the poem is not primarily an idea or an image, or a series of ideas and images, but a memory of this specific sequence of words, a memory suffused by the qualities of my experience of them—and, paradoxical as it may sound, this memory may remain even when I have forgotten the words themselves. As long as I retain a memory of the "form" of the words, of how they happened, and happened to me, in a certain order, and with certain effects, I retain something of the poem. This aspect of the poem is inseparable from the deep pleasure which animates both my reading of it and the internal representation of it which I keep, a pleasure which no summary of the poem would convey, however faithful it might be to the meaning of its words.

How, then, can we address the question of form in "The actual Dialogue"? A familiar move would be to essay a formal description of the poem, and from there to examine the function of each of the identified formal properties in the reader's experience. We could note the repetitions of phrases and of sounds; we could scan the poem; we could tabulate the grammatical strength of end-stoppings (observing, for instance, that they all correspond to syntactic divisions of one kind or other). According to the paradoxical sense of form that operates in literary criticism, we could consider the phonic material of the sounds themselves, such as the echoed vowels -ear, -igh, and -are, or the repeated /b/ and /f/ sounds. Then we could try to correlate this array of formal features with the meaning and the emotional quality we find in the poem, and try, too, to explain why this correlation produces in the reader (or at least in some readers) a powerful response.[7]

Such an account would turn the poem into an aesthetic object, where "form" and "content" remain separate, but refer endlessly to one another. It ignores the fact that we apprehend these so-called "formal" features as *already meaningful*, and meaningful in a particular context. It overlooks the eventness of the literary work, which means that form needs to be understood verbally—as "taking form," or "forming," or even "losing form." And it presents a model of poetic response as an entirely generalizable process, in which the poem is understood as part of the network of cultural codes and not as a challenge to them. Not surprisingly, most commentators today—outside the introductory poetry class—would prefer to talk about South African history and politics, the "black consciousness" movement of the 1970s, the much-touted government strategy of "dialogue," the discourse of racism, the conventional metaphorization of black and white, the allusion to Langston Hughes,[8] the situation of Serote as a black writer in South Africa, and so on. All this would be valuable, but would also fail to explain why the experience of reading the poem can be so remarkable.

As with a formal description, this contextual and semantic description could apply equally well to a poem with little power and little memorability. What has to be shown is how in the writing of this poem all such "contextual" material is worked into a unique formal event which a given reader may experience as a powerful, and powerfully pleasurable, encounter with alterity. In this way, social contradictions—as Adorno understood—are manifested at the level of form.

There is no question, in fact, of defining the singularity of the poem by drawing around it a line that separates it from something that might be called its "context." Context is already there in the words— in so far as they are words and not sounds or shapes—and it is already there in my response, in so far as I respond as a culturally constituted human individual and not a physiological apparatus or a sophisticated computer. In fact, singularity is *constituted* by what we might call "contextual" operations; it is not a matter of some inviolable core at the heart of all accessible meaning, but is the product of a set of contexts bearing down upon a here and now—contexts which include the language, the literary tradition, generic properties, and cultural norms, and which construct the reading of the poem by constructing both poem and reader. Meaning is therefore not something that appears in defining opposition or complementary apposition to form, as it is conceived of in the aesthetic tradition, but as something already taken up within form; forms are made out of meanings quite as much as they are made out of sounds and shapes. Form and meaning both happen, and are part of the same happening.

To yoke form to singularity and to include meaning within form in this way is to go against one of the strongest elements in the semantic field and history of the term: its association with generality and transcendence (by contrast with the specificity frequently associated with "content" or "meaning"). It is no doubt this sense of serene abstraction from the give-and-take of contingent, meaning-charged reality that makes the subject of form so suspect to the politically or historically inclined critic. Form in the sense I am opposing is that which can be apprehended by the mind without mediation, whether one thinks of it as existing in a Platonic beyond or an Aristotelian entelechy; it is transparent, pure, abstractable, generalizable. The traditional notion of literary form—or form in general—leaves little room for the operation of otherness. (The paradox I mentioned earlier, whereby the physical material of language—acoustic and visual—is also treated under the rubric of form, does not introduce singularity into the picture, since these physical properties are themselves treated as generalizable.)

One way of responding to Serote's poem as a formally singular work is to write a commentary on the experience of performing it, in the sense developed in the previous chapter, as a reader. (I mean by this a specific reader, not an ideal or average one; my own reading is colored by my personal history—most significantly, my upbringing as a white male South African.) Such a commentary would not separate forming from meaning, or from the registering of singularity and welcoming of alterity. I have been emphasizing that the "experience" of alterity and singularity may not always be a conscious one, and it is quite possible that certain elements in the poem—that is, in my performance of it—which contribute to its power for me do not register on my consciousness. By the same token, however, my attempt to describe that performance may convey, without my knowing, something of what I remain unaware. For the sake of space, I confine myself to some of the things I find myself wanting to say about the opening lines of the poem.

"Do not fear Baas": the four words come from nowhere, or from the darkness of my pre-poem anticipation, unannounced, unlocated, unidentified; before I take them in as a statement, they brush against me in the dark as the physical signal of another human presence. Yet when I understand them as a meaningful sequence, they offer reassurance, seeming to know in advance the alarm that they will cause, and offer to allay it even as they produce it. The monosyllabic words are simple, and so is the syntax which connects them, as if spoken to a child, or spoken in a language that is not native to the speaker. Yet the register is uncolloquially formal. Somewhere in the background, further complicating the tonality, hovers the angelic utterance, "Fear not."

But it is not reassuring to have one's fears predicted, mapped out, at least not by the source of those fears. I have been seen, and seen through, while I remain in the dark. "Baas," the universal South African word for "master" or "sir" (an Afrikaans word derived from an identical word in Dutch, itself the source of the American English word "boss"), the word of deference, the word that claims to do homage to me (for I am immediately interpellated by this word as a white man living in South Africa) rings with a dangerous hollowness, coming as it does without pause after this demonstration of pre-emptive superiority. It is a word whose massive potential for satire I, as the white master, am not allowed, or not able, to perceive, yet it is hard to take it at face value when it is linked to an imperative, in a situation in which the addressee does not feel in charge. And yet there's nothing in the words to cancel their positive meaning, the offer of goodwill which they present. If that offer is genuinely there, I cannot afford to miss it, to lose it in the darkness of my fears. Too much is at stake—at its fullest extent, the future of the country in which the encounter is taking place. The appellation "Baas" can be quite affectionate, and how am I to know how much, if any, positive feeling it carries here? For all their immediacy, the words remain alien, resistant, irreducible; they have no depth, no underside; I can only read them again, go round the possibilities of tone, register, and implication one more time.

As words in a written poem, of course, they are not spoken, and each time I speak them I have to choose a particular tone, setting a limit to the range of nuances that play across them. As I speak them in my chosen voice, however, I am aware of that range, even if I cannot vocalize it in a single utterance. This remains true of the following lines. "It's just that I appeared": words of explanation and comfort, yet conveying the alarm of an encounter with an apparition, emerging suddenly out of nowhere—the nowhere that people of "other" races inhabit in a racist culture. "And our faces met": what could be simpler and more calming. Yet at the same time there is something disturbing about the notion of faces, rather than people, meeting. There is a nakedness here, on both sides; we are worlds away from Prufrock preparing a face to meet the faces that you meet. How heartening the embrace of that "our," underlining the shared humanity of the two figures in the drama, very different from the face that devastates the Levinasian subject. Yet how worrying, too, that no distinction can be drawn between us, that whatever subservience the word "Baas" signaled seems to have evaporated. Then comes the culmination of the reassurance which is also the culmination of the rising sense of alarm: "In this black night that's like me."

The repetition of "Do not fear" is, in the traditional sense, a formal feature of the poem: one might say that its five occurrences provide the work with a structural frame. But to put it that way is to minimize the effectiveness of these repetitions in the unfolding of the utterance, which function temporally, not spatially. When I encounter the words for the second time, I sense that we are even further removed from conversation: there is a hint of something like a lullaby, heightened as the words come back again and again in a refrain. By being repeated, the sound and rhythm of the phrase are increasingly foregrounded (though always as the conveyer of meaning, never as sheer sonic material), and this move toward the domain of song contributes to my experience of being comforted. After the second "Do not fear" I again expect some amplification, some reason why fear would be out of place. The next line seems as if it might be leading to such an amplification—"We will always meet . . . "—only to give me, over the hesitation of the line break, one more reason to fear—"When you do not expect me." And then another repetition, a re-lacing of words heard earlier increases the intensity of the threat: "I will appear, / In the night that's black like me."

But I am not the addressee, I remind myself; the work is a staging of the linguistic event it involves me in. I put myself in the addressee's place—no, the poem puts me in that place—but I also deduce, construct, an addressee who is not me, a white South African man, out alone after dark, almost anywhere in that country, startled by an encounter with a black person—probably a man, too—whom he does not know.[9] I am and I am not that man as I read the poem. Serote's words are neither reassurance nor threat; they stage these impulses as events. The rest of the poem, which I will not discuss here, plays out a generous attempt to comprehend (in both senses) the fears on both sides, though it can hardly be said to offer a prescription for racial harmony. My knowledge that these words were written by a black South African in the early 1970s is part of my response, and as I read them I experience that event of writing, within but also in opposition to a predominantly white, European, tradition of poetry, a tradition from which it has borrowed its appearance on the page and its economically organized and shaped language; against that background the poem itself makes an unexpected and threatening appearance, an other that changes me as I perform it.

This is not a matter of placing the poem in a context, but of allowing that context to move in and through the poem, enriching or darkening the words as they take their effect. The poem does not leave its writing behind, to be deduced from it, historicized and biographized; it *is* writing, a writing, that I perform and experience every time I read it, every time I offer a reading of it. The racism that the poem probes, challenges, mocks, and seeks to overcome is brought into being anew, and a terrible history reborn, each time it is creatively performed by a reader. There may, it is true, be readers for whom the troubling energies of racist ways of being so evident in our societies are not a live issue, and for them the poem would be a largely historical exercise; but this is a possibility that obtains for every work of art.

Responding responsibly to Serote's poem as a critic, then, means producing a commentary that stages the act of reading it—not in the sense of reporting what happens as it is read, but of bringing out as far as possible in the writing of the commentary the singularity of the experience of reading for a given reader, a singularity that lies in its resistance to the very interpretive methods that give it its existence. Such a commentary will itself be a singular act-event, registering the here and now of the reader while it attempts to do justice to the otherness of the poem. It must simultaneously bring the poem as other into the field of the same—so that readers for whom it is a blank can begin to appreciate it—and affirm and sustain its otherness—so that readers can register its power. The commentary itself, therefore, must strive to be a singular and inventive event, and thereby invite readings that respond inventively to its own singularity and inventiveness.

Form and instrumentalism

What difference does this way of conceiving of literature make to our understanding of the traditional notion of "literary form"? The properties which have gone under that name—sound-patterns, rhythm, syntactic variation, narrative construction, and so on—are precisely what call forth the performative response I have been delineating.[10] The work's references—to history, to shared codes, to psychological states— in themselves invite only a referential reading; its moral pronouncements invite only a behavioral—or perhaps spiritual—response; its encoding of intention invites only a biographical reading; and so on. But when the language which establishes these relations to the extratextual is significantly organized, when it has salient qualities which are not exhausted by these functions, we can say that they are being performed, that every reference out is also, and in the same gesture, a reference in, that every metaphor is also a staging of metaphoricity, every embodied intention an enactment of intentionality.

The effect of this mobilization of meaning by formal properties is that the text can never close down on a represented world, can never become solely the reflection of or a pointer to a set of existents outside language. The question of meaning and referring is kept alive *as a question*; referentiality is enacted—but not simply endorsed—in every literary act. The literary work thus has available to it all the resources of meaningful language—it can describe, prove, evoke, cajole, move, warn, persuade, promise, or narrate in the most concrete and convincing manner—without suffering the limitations imposed on purely instrumental language by the purposes which it must serve. (The one requirement that remains, perhaps, is the need to produce pleasure, and this pleasure, in so far as it is literary, is brought about precisely by the performative, or more accurately the performing and performed, dimension of literature.)

Once we identify the uniqueness of the literary work with its singular performative mobility it becomes difficult to approach it in a purely instrumental way, or at least it becomes evident how an instrumentality not founded upon a response to this singularity fails in its responsibility to the text and to the institution of literature. An instrumental approach seeks not only to comprehend the text by relating it to known and fixed parameters and values, but to generalize its uniqueness and transform its performativity into a static and therefore usable paradigm. What literary form does is to produce (in conjunction, of course, with the assumptions and conventions of the literary institution which govern reading at a particular historical moment) a suspension of linguistic instrumentality, a blocking of the aesthetic urge to separate form from content and to assign content alone to the domain of ethics and politics. It is form without formalism.[11] Which means, of course, that we can hardly go on using the term "form," unless we do so with conscious paleonymic intention. The sounds and shapes of the text are always already meaningful sounds and shapes, and there is no moment, not even a theoretical one, at which it is possible to isolate a purely formal property—at least not without turning the literary work into something else.

It follows that acts of literature do not operate directly upon the political realm. When literary works are politically effective in a direct way—Shelley's *Mask of Anarchy*, say, or Tressell's *Ragged-Trousered Philanthropists*—it is not their literariness that is crucial but some other quality or qualities, such as rhetorical or argumentative effectiveness, vividness of description or emotive appeal, or imaginative modeling of utopian projects. But literature can act powerfully to hold the political and the ethical up for scrutiny by momentarily dissociating them from their usual pressing context, *performing* the ethical decision and the political gesture. Literature—when it is responded to as literature—is not a political instrument, yet it is deeply implicated in the political. In its blocking of both the conventionally aesthetic and the instrumental, the literary work fails to answer to our habitual needs in processing language; it thus estranges itself, presents itself as simultaneously familiar and other, puts us under a certain obligation (to attend scrupulously, to suspend as far as we can our usual assumptions and practices, to translate the work into our terms while remaining aware of the necessary betrayal that this involves). To respond fully to a literary work is to be responsively and responsibly aware of that otherness, and of the demands it makes upon us.

It might be objected that to stress the importance in literary invention of form in this sense, of otherness and verbal singularity, is to privilege certain genres and modes, and certain periods, over others—poetry over prose, avant-garde art over more conventional art, and the modernist period over earlier periods, in particular. To make this objection is to misunderstand the nature of alterity as it operates in the artistic sphere. Linguistic and formal inventiveness represents only one kind of literary inventiveness, a kind we associate especially with poetry and with modernism (although of course there are many novels and plays, and many works in all periods, that bring about their literary effects through these types of inventiveness). Many other kinds of inventiveness occur: a work that is largely conventional in style and language—a novel by Smollett or Trollope, say—may be extremely powerful in its apprehension of unfamiliar modes of feeling, its elaboration of hitherto unexplored aspects of human relationships, its crystallization of new ideas. What makes these works literary works (as distinct from other kinds of text that have been inventively productive in such areas) is that these new understandings or feelings depend on the works' specific use of language and come into existence in the event of performance. Although they may change the way people think and feel, their particular newness, which is to say their literariness, can be experienced only in this event.

Nevertheless, it has remained true throughout the history of Western culture that the artists whose work has been received as the most powerful, the most intensely pleasure-giving, the most lastingly valued, have almost invariably been those who have inventively re-created the cultural fabric by formal as well as by other means. Any created work or body of works that we prize for its singularity—whether the achievement of an individual or of a group—we are also prizing for its inventiveness, that is to say, for its introduction of alterity, both in its time (acknowledged or unacknowledged) and in ours. From the Homeric epics to the poetry of Ted Hughes, from the tragedies of Aeschylus to the plays of Caryl Churchill, from the dialogues of Plato to the fiction of Toni Morrison, what we recognize and enjoy as the unique configurations of language, the individual deployment of the rich cultural materials that—in our different and changing ways—we share, are always inventive welcomings of the other.

Responsibility and ethics 9

Responsibility for the other

Affirming the other, the new, in all the different modalities I have considered in this book, including the invention of the work of art and the just response to it, makes demands. Creatively responding to the other, we have seen, involves the shifting of ingrained modes of understanding in order to take account of that which was systematically excluded by them. Attentiveness to what is outside the familiar requires effort, even if it is the effort of resisting effortful behavior, of emptying out the too full, excessively goal-oriented consciousness. What drives and directs this effort? We can talk about motivation in terms of the pleasures and rewards to be gained from creating a work that is original and influential, or from doing justice in a creative response to the uniqueness of a person or an artifact, but motivation of this sort accounts only for the wish to be inventive, and does not seem enough to account for what actually happens. The act, it seems, springs from a hard-to-explain commitment to the other, to the new, to that which is coming into being.

One way of describing this attitude is to say that the other—whether the other I struggle to create or the other I encounter in the shape of a person or a work—arouses in me a sense of *responsibility*. We may make a distinction between two kinds of responsibility in this situation: responsibility *to* the other and responsibility *for* the other. (Substituting a near synonym makes the difference even clearer: to be answerable *to* someone is not the same as being answerable *for* him or her.) Although there is a sense in which I am responsible to the other—the other calls me to account, I answer to it as best I can—this is nowhere near as demanding as my responsibility for the other. Being responsible for the other involves assuming the other's needs (if only the need to exist), affirming it, sustaining it, being prepared to give up my own wants and satisfactions for the sake of the other.

Although responsibility is a concept we employ for our dealings with a wide range of entities, including persons, cultures, and the natural environment, it is not one generally used of artistic creations.[1] It provides, however, a useful way of indicating the strange compulsion involved in creative behavior, a compulsion that is manifested in a minor way as I grope for sentences to articulate ideas or let a favorite poem work freshly upon me, and more consequentially in major acts of inventiveness, verbal or otherwise. It is a compulsion that leads to risk, a crucial concept in any consideration of creativity. Since there can be no certainty in opening oneself to the other—certainty being by definition excluded—every such opening is a gamble. I trust the other before I know what the other will bring.[2] It may be the best, it may be the worst. I take responsibility for the other before any calculation—for the risk is incalculable. (We noted in Chapter 4 that although there are many ways in which a culture may benefit from the inventive practice of art, there is always a possibility that it could instead be damaged or destroyed.) I cherish the other, not in spite of but *because* of its otherness, since its otherness is precisely what makes it valuable to me, and, without any guarantees, I undertake to realize and sustain this otherness as fully and enduringly as possible—which means being prepared to start all over again with each fresh encounter.

What we experience in responding to the artwork, however, is not a generalized obligation but a call coming from the work itself—the work as singular staging of otherness. We have already seen what this means. The text that functions powerfully as literature (rather than as exhortation, description, mystification, and so on) uses the materials of the same—the culture which it and the reader inhabit and within which they are constituted—in such a way as to open onto that which cannot be accounted for by those materials (though they have in fact made possible its emergence). And the response to such a work—the responsible response, the one that attempts to apprehend the other as other—is a performance of it that, while it inevitably strives to convert the other into the same, strives also to allow the same to be modified by the other.

Such a reading does not, however, aim only to appropriate and interpret the work, to bring it into the familiar circle, but also to register its resistance and irreducibility, and to register it in such a way as to dramatize what it is about familiar modes of understanding that render them unable to accommodate this stranger. Otherness in this sense is not necessarily something hidden; it may lie entirely on the surface, uncannily familiar but prohibiting appropriation and domestication. And it is always otherness as a relation to the familiar; indeed, as we have seen, it would be more accurate to say that it is precisely this relation, or relating, which is being staged in the performance of the inventive work of art. Taking responsibility for the work includes being responsible and responsive to the culture within which we encounter it, the culture which it offers to remake in some way, slight or momentous.

Certain kinds of support and succor for other persons are enjoined by conventional moral codes, but my responsibility for the other person *as other* is more demanding than these requirements. My obligation is to refashion what I think and what I am in order to take the fullest possible account of, to respect, safeguard, and learn from, the otherness and singularity of the other, and to do so without any certainty about the consequences of my act. The same is true of the products of human creativity (and of that creativity itself): a responsible response to an inventive work of art, science, or philosophy (to mention only a few possibilities) is one that brings it into being anew by allowing it, in a performance of its singularity for me, for my place and time, to refigure the ways in which I, and my culture, think and feel. This may mean being willing to take on trust that it has something valuable to say when it appears obscure or objectionable, at least until several readings—and perhaps conversations or research—make an informed and just response possible. (We are more likely to be patient with such a work when we have reason to believe that our initial response will only be temporary; when, for instance, it has been recommended by someone whose judgment we respect or it is by an author whose other works we have come to enjoy as inventive.)

Responsibility for the other is not *additional* to the traditional requirement of responsiveness discussed in Chapter 6. Unlike responsiveness to physical stimuli, responsiveness to the other must involve something like responsibility because the other cannot come into existence unless it is affirmed, welcomed, trusted, nurtured (even though, as we have seen, coming into existence necessarily involves ceasing to be other). Responsibility for the other is a form of hospitality and generosity.[3] Furthermore, in responsibility I respond with much more than my cognitive faculties: my emotional and sometimes my physical self are also at stake. Hence the risk involved, the risk implicit in any act of hospitality—I am obliged to affirm something with all that I am before I know what it is, before, in fact, it is. Although I have been talking of a "sense" of responsibility, and of responsibility as an "attitude," these words are too weak: responsibility for the other is not so much a feeling I experience as a situation I find myself in; it is what constitutes me as a literary reader.

Responsibility of this kind may often look like irresponsibility, but responsibility of any other kind—responsibility based on the calculation of likely outcomes, for instance—is something our computers could do for us. There is no straightforward chronology here: this is one of the ways in which invention does not conform to the normal protocols of causality. Only in accepting responsibility for the other do I bring it—or let it come—into existence; and there is a sense in which the responsibility precedes even the "I" that is said to "accept" it, since the act always remakes the actor.

Ethics

Responsibility is an ethical term; it implies an "ought." To be responsible for the other as it comes into being (and thus bring it into being) is to be under an obligation to it; to respond responsibly to the otherness of a literary work is to do justice to it; treating literature as literature means being hospitable and generous: my entire discussion to this point has been shot through with ethical considerations. This raises fresh problems for my account of invention, creation, and responsiveness. What is the ethical ground for attention to and affirmation of otherness, when the result of this effort may be without any humanly recognizable merit, or indeed—since the other that is brought into being may, as I have suggested, turn out to be a monstrosity—may serve quite inhuman ends?[4]

We can only continue to use terms with ethical implications like "responsibility" and "obligation"—indeed "ethics" itself—if we are prepared to make some kind of distinction between the most fundamental ethical demands, which always involve unpredictability and risk, and specific obligations governing concrete situations in a given social context, which require the greatest possible control of outcomes. To the latter, the name "morality" is often given.[5] There is no necessary correlation between a responsible openness to the other as I compose music or respond to another person or read a novel and the obligations I have under the moral codes embodied in social norms, religious institutions, the law of my country, and, probably, my own superego. This is not to say that these two kinds of obligation are unrelated; on the contrary, a moral code, legal system, or political program may be called ethical if it is informed by something like the responsibility that I have sketched, even though it will always be tested and exceeded by such a responsibility.

Not only is there no moral or pragmatic ground for responsibility, there is also no philosophical ground. The ethical force that conditions the creative act is ungrounded—here Levinas's difficult thinking is valuable—because it is *prior to* any possible grounds. Without responsibility for the other, as we have seen, there would be no other; with no other, repeatedly appearing, always different, there would be no same, no self, no society, no morality. We cannot deduce the obligation to the other from the existing world; the existing world—including the means by which any deductions could be made about ethics or responsibility—is premised upon an obligation to the other. Ethics, then, is the fundamental relation not just between subjects but also between the subject and its multiple others—a relation that is not a relation and that cannot be named, for it is logically prior to relations and names, prior in fact to logic. *We find ourselves already responsible for the other*—and this fact constitutes the artistic sphere as much as it does the ethical. This is part of what we mean when we say invention, alterity, and singularity are *events*: they happen to us.

It may be objected that this use of terms like "responsibility" and "ethics," lumping together kindness to other people, artistic creation, and acts of reading, is so broad in its compass as to empty them of any useful meaning. In particular, it might be said to dissipate the terms' real force, which can be sustained only if we recognize the primacy of interpersonal relations in the deployment of any such vocabulary. This criticism has a certain validity and might lead to the use of different terms, terms not already saturated with humanistic moral implications, were it not for the fact that it is precisely in invoking a long tradition of thought that "ethics," "responsibility," and the like are particularly useful. For the claim implicit in using them is that the current discussion of alterity is both a disruption and a continuation of an ancient discourse: as always, we bring the new into being by refashioning the old rather than by jettisoning it. In Chapter 2, we examined the parallels between responding to the other in the process of creation and responding to the other in the form of a person; in both, respect for the singularity of the other involves a willingness to have the grounds of one's thinking recast and renewed.

The ethical responsibility for the other that, I am arguing, is at the heart of creativity has often been articulated, in different terms and different contexts, more or less fully and coherently, many times in human history. The present argument is an attempt to derive from some parts of this long tradition an account of the issues appropriate for my time and place. I am not making any claims about the relative importance of the different manifestations of the ethical relation that I have discussed; clearly, it is right that moral or political judgment should place the responsibility for human beings above responsibility for their products and measure creativity by its benefits to humanity (or to some other category). But the special value of a non-moral discourse of ethics is that it can provide insights into the fundamental conditions of the moral-political domain, the world of rules, programs, categories, without being reduced to them.

The ethics of literature

Responding responsibly to a work of art means attempting to do justice to it as a singular other; it involves a judgment that is not simply ethical or aesthetic, and that does not attempt to pigeonhole it or place it on a scale of values, but that operates as an affirmation of the work's ˉinventiveness. We might compare it to the response of a judge in a courtroom, whose initial responsibility is to assess a particular case by bringing to bear on it all the relevant legal history and documentation, and thus to dissipate its uniqueness by relating it to the general field of the law. However, to be said to act justly he or she then has to move beyond any calculation which could be made in terms of the codes of legal practice, and to act with a decisiveness that no machine could emulate. Only in so doing is the act truly responsible, truly responsive to the singularity of the case (remembering always that this singularity is not an inviolable identity outside codes and conventions but is produced through them).

It is this singularity (which, since singularity is always that which resists or exceeds existing frameworks, is also otherness) that makes a demand on the judge, as judge. No justice is possible without the singularity of the case—and of the individual standing trial—being so affirmed (and only, it might be added, in similar acts of affirmation throughout daily existence can just or ethical social life prevail). To act morally toward other persons entails, it hardly needs saying, as full an attempt at understanding them and their situation as one is capable of; yet both the primary claim of another person upon one and the final measure of one's behavior lies in the response to, and affirmation of, the otherness which resists that understanding. Practically, of course, this leads to all the problems of interpersonal and intercultural ethics that we are familiar with; how, for instance, do we balance the right of another culture to employ its own practices against the demands of the ethical law we honor and assume to be universal in its reach? Respect for otherness does not inhibit intervention in the affairs of others, but it does away with any thought that there might be an algorithmic solution to such problems. They can only be addressed as specific and singular cases.[6]

It may sound as though there can be only one response that does full justice to a singular other, including a work of art. This is not so, and not only because the obligation is always to do justice to the other in a particular context, which means different responses are appropriate in different times and places. Even if we consider a given individual responding to a work in a given situation, there are many ways to do justice to it: were there only one, it would have to be in some sense deducible from the work, the individual, and the context. There is no difference between this logic and the logic governing the invention of a work: an artist's response to prevailing conditions and previous inventions, if it is creative rather than mechanical, is, as we have noted, far from being the only possible one. Nevertheless, the *experience* of an inventive work or response to a work is usually one of rightness, as if no other alternative could have succeeded.

To read a literary work responsibly, then, is to read it without placing over it a grid of possible uses, as historical evidence, moral lesson, path to truth, political inspiration, or personal encouragement, and without passing judgment on the work or its author (although in other contexts it may be vital to make such judgments). It is to trust in the unpredictability of reading, its openness to the future. From this reading, of course, a responsible instrumentality may follow, perhaps one with modified methods or goals. And to the extent that reading literary criticism or philosophy or history partakes of the experience of the literary, the same is true: a preparedness to be challenged by the work, an alertness to its singular otherness, an attentiveness to the way it operates through mobile and meaningful forms as well as by thematic representation and conceptual argument, will result in a fuller, more responsible response, and in an enhanced possibility of change in the future. The ethics of literary reading is less a matter of the exercise of a certain kind of effort on each reading—though it is that (including the effort of disencumbering the reading self)—than a disposition, a habit, a way of being in the world of words. There is no necessary correlation between being a good reader, in this sense, and being a good person, just as there is no necessary correlation between being a good artist and being a good person; nevertheless, some of the same values are at work in both spheres.

All creative shapings of language (and any other cultural materials) make demands that can, in this extended sense, be called ethical. To find oneself reading an inventive work is to find oneself subject to certain obligations—to respect its otherness, to respond to its singularity, to avoid reducing it to the familiar and the utilitarian even while attempting to comprehend it by relating it to these. The distinctive ethical demand made by the literary work is not to be identified with its characters or its plot, with the human intercourse and judgments it portrays, with its depictions of virtues and vices or of the difficulty of separating these; all these can be found in other discourses, such as historical writing or journalistic reporting. It is not a question of literature's capacity to provide a moral education; that too is a property it shares with other kinds of writing.[7] Rather, it is to be found in what makes it literature: its staging of the fundamental processes whereby language works upon us and upon the world. The literary work demands a reading that does justice to the formal elaboration of these processes, a reading in the sense of a performance, a putting-into-action or putting-into-play that involves both active engagement and a letting-go, a hospitable embrace of the other.

There is thus an ethical dimension to any act of literary signification, and there is also a sense in which the formally innovative work, the one that most estranges itself from the reader, makes the most sharply challenging (which is not to say the most profound) ethical demand. Formal innovation (of the sort that matters in literature) is a testing of the operations of meaning, and is therefore a kind of ethical experimentation. To respond to the demand of the literary work as the demand of the other is to attend to it as a unique event whose happening is a call, a challenge, an obligation: understand how little you understand me, translate my untranslatability, learn me by heart and thus learn the otherness that inhabits the heart.[8] It means suspending all those carefully applied codes and conventions and reinventing them, as if this work brought them into being even while it proved them limited in their scope. Levinas writes of the relation to the other as that of hostage to captor, emphasizing the randomness with which I feel myself summoned by the other—not because I am who I am but because I happen to be in a particular place and time.[9]

But the other is also vulnerable, in need of my protection, "destitute," to use Levinas's word. Its power lies in its weakness. Literature, for all the force which it is capable of exercising, can achieve nothing without readers—responsible readers. (There is, of course, a certain force exercised by a work, and by a way of reading works, that may serve to sustain and strengthen a reader's existing modes of understanding and feeling: my rather specialized use of the term "literature" would not extend to such a text or way of reading. Other critics— I mentioned Richards earlier—have used terms like "stock response" and "sentimentality" to characterize this type of writing and this type of response.) Lest this all sound somewhat severe, let me repeat my claim that it is in this apprehension of otherness and in the demands it makes that the peculiar pleasure of the literary response (over and above the pleasure to be gained from new information, sensuous patterning, stirring of memory, moral exemplification, and so on) is to be experienced.

An everyday impossibility 10

I began the main part of this book with a self-reflexive gesture, with my attempt to describe the act of writing *in* the act of writing, as a minor example of possible inventiveness. Yet the terms in which I have described the inventive event, the just response to the singularity of the other in the act of bringing it into the field of the same, and the consequent alteration of the mental and emotional ground on which the subject and the culture stand, may make it sound like an extraordinarily arduous and rarely accomplished task. How can this sense of an exceptional event be squared with my claim that invention happens all the time—that countless works of art exhibit inventiveness, as do an even larger number of other events of writing, speaking, gesturing, and even thinking?

In one sense invention *is* extraordinary, in that it is a moment that resists explanation in terms of the rules that govern the ordinary. It is always a miracle. And for the same reason, we can never observe it as it happens. But we can deduce from the multiplicity of inventive effects that it is not extraordinary in the sense of "uncommon." If in my discussion invention has come to sound like a highly infrequent event of considerable magnitude, this impression is in part the result of the inevitable magnification that occurs when fleeting experiences are described at length and mulled over in detail. It is also the result of a misjudgment about the mind.

There is a widely shared illusion that humanity's accumulated knowledge amounts to a healthy proportion of what there is to know—not many people would be prepared to put a figure on it, but we speak and act as if it were well over the halfway mark. Yet the history of the accumulation of knowledge and the confidence of its holders suggests that a better estimate would be a tiny fraction, if, that is, the process is not an endless one. The mind and the mind's products are not exempt from this illusion. The vast body of commentary about artworks from earlier centuries and about the processes whereby they have been created and received, a body of commentary that we take to be somewhere near complete, may in fact only scratch the surface of the works and the richly detailed, complexly organized mental systems and procedures that make them possible. We talk and write as if a fairly large proportion of what can be pertinently stated about—to take an example at random—*A Midsummer Night's Dream* has already been stated. But if there can be no end to cultural change, there is no end to what can be said about *A Midsummer Night's Dream* and found to be valuable. Everything that has been said so far amounts to little more than nothing. Hindsight allows us to see how inventive artists have exploited the state of the language, of generic forms of their time, and of the wider cultural context, by finding opportunities hidden to others; but we can learn no lesson from this except that it is impossible to foretell what such artists will do in the future. The potential of any medium is infinite, as long as the cultural milieu from which it springs continues to be different for each generation.

When full account is taken of the fact that both the mind and many of its products are highly complex and constantly changing fields of interrelated forces, possibilities, nodes, and tendencies, it becomes easier to acknowledge the everydayness of creativity and inventiveness, occurring on a scale that reaches from the minute to the monumental. When I speak of the habitual frames whereby we process the world being altered by a singular performance, I do not mean that everything suddenly looks different. For example, one creative response to an instance of singular otherness is laughter: an explosive, physico-psychological affirmation of a person's or a work's inventive juxtaposition or fusion of cultural materials. Although there exist many explanations of laughter, none can account for it to the extent of being able to predict when and where it will happen—and this is not merely because of the inadequacy of our analytical tools, but because laughter is entirely dependent upon unpredictability. A laugh is an eventful response to a singular event.

Virtually any mode of writing may be inventive, any variety of artistic creation, any philosophical or mathematical thought, any scientific advance, the reading of any text, even any pragmatic conceptualization in politics or personal relations. An unpremeditated act—a deed of generosity, the movement of a surgeon's hand, a stroke in a ball game—can be a creative event. The other that is brought into being by an artist in a moment of invention, though it may be something as ambitious as a new way of perceiving nature or of understanding love, may also be something as slight as a different handling of the heroic couplet or an unprecedented type of rhyme. One realizes that creative, responsible responsiveness to the other is not a rare phenomenon but part of the texture of daily life. Levinas was fond of giving as an instance of ethics in practice the "After you" whereby I invite someone to go through a door before me. This example is clearly provocative, but it can be taken seriously: the minimal acknowledgment of the other implicit in a gracious expression of deference may have in it a grain of ethics, an ever-so-slight creative impulse—perhaps the discovery of a gesture or an expression that pleases and reassures my companion not as a familiar fellow human being but, for me in this instant, as the singular other.

There is a strict sense in which the inventive event, for all its everydayness, is impossible: the irruption of the other into the same does not, and cannot, sit comfortably within any of the explanatory frameworks by which we characterize the possible. This is what I mean by calling it a miracle, though of course without any religious implications. The most ingenious explanation will always turn out to fall short of the central fact that has to be accounted for: something new, what I have been calling "the other," comes into the humanly constituted and constituting cultural sphere and changes it. The other may be psychologized, in terms of material held in the preconscious and the unconscious; sociologized, in terms of dimly perceived cultural inheritances; or theologized, in terms of divine intervention. None of these explanations or any others, whatever their validity, can claim predictive ability; they cannot state in advance when or how an inventive act is to take place, who will be inventive, or what the invention will consist of. This is not because such discourses lack the necessary power and precision but because an invention that could be fully accounted for, that could be programmed and predicted, would not be an invention. The discourses at our disposal may provide a way of understanding virtually everything about an inventive act—its psychic ingredients, its cultural matrix, its etiology and teleology—but they will leave unanswered the crucial question: how does the new, the other, come into being when all we have is what we have? As Steiner puts it, "How is it possible to think new?"—a question, he notes, that is "one of the most challenging in epistemology," yet one that has received "only transient, often conventional notice."[1]

I have attempted in the foregoing chapters to develop an interrelated set of terms to enable fruitful discussion of this question. It will be evident that their meanings and usefulness depend on those interrelations. The *singularity* of the artwork is not simply a matter of difference from other works (what I term "uniqueness"), but a transformative difference, a difference, that is to say, that involves the irruption of *otherness* or *alterity* into the cultural field. And this combination of singularity and alterity is further specified by *inventiveness*: the work comes into being, through an act that is also an event, as an *authored* entity. Among all the inventions that can be so characterized, works of art are distinctive in the demand they make for a *performance*, a performance in which the authored singularity, alterity, and inventiveness of the work as an exploitation of the multiple powers of language are experienced and affirmed in the present, in a creative, responsible reading. But performance in this sense, I have argued, is a matter both of performing and being performed by the work: hence the *eventness* of the reading—and thus of the work—is crucial.

Although I have emphasized that any inventive work of art, by introducing otherness into the field of the same, reshapes cultural norms and habits as well as what I have called idiocultures, I have said little about the content of that reshaping, and why it should be valued. The history of aesthetic thought contains many claims about what it is that original art (as opposed to mere novelty) brings into the world, and it may seem odd that I have refrained from making such claims. I have said only that inventiveness can be known (and by implication valued) as such if it makes more inventiveness possible. Why is this a desirable process?

The answer lies in the relation of alterity to the field which it transforms. The otherness that enters a culture through an invention (whether artistic or otherwise) is, I have argued, not a pre-existing entity somewhere outside of, and unrelated to, what is known. Rather, it manifests itself as an event of reshaping, ranging from the major to the minuscule, brought about by an individual's or group's exploitation of a culture's contradictions, overdeterminations, marginalizations, gaps, and tensions.[2] In coming to be acknowledged—which means in the process of shifting frameworks so that it can be acknowledged—the other exposes a reality or truth of which the culture and its subjects were unaware, and unaware for reasons that are far from arbitrary. This uncovered reality may be pleasant; it may equally be unpalatable or even dangerous. Its occlusion is likely to be in the interest of those in power, and, as the history of censorship shows, it may be politically unacceptable to state authorities. What value it might have cannot be measured in utilitarian terms. Yet the revelation of the hidden costs of a culture's stability, the bringing to fruitfulness of seeds that had lain dormant, the opening-up of possibilities that had remained closed, is—however risky—a good in itself, particularly when the process is a continuous one, allowing no permanent settling of norms and habits, and therefore no single structure of dominance and exclusion.

The ethics of invention makes impossible demands. Not only is it impossible to conceive of the other for which I am responsible in terms that would allow me to know in advance what my responsibility amounts to, but I also have numerous—indeed, infinite—responsibilities, all of which are absolute and immediate in their demands. Yet responsible inventions occur every day, not just in spite of this multiple impossibility but also in a sense because of it. If it were possible to have a purely conceptual knowledge of the other as singular other, to predict or produce its arrival, neither otherness nor inventiveness would exist. If I could calculate, apportion, and satisfy all my responsibilities, there would be no such thing as responsibility or ethics. And if literary works and our responses to them could be programmed in advance, inventive literature and literary criticism would cease to be.

I am not able to offer a recipe for a new mode of criticism, therefore: the best commentaries on literary works have always surprised us with their singularity and inventiveness, and will always do so. I am suggesting, however, that the attempt to do justice to literary works as *events*, welcoming alterity, countersigning the singular signature of the artist, inventively responding to invention, combined with a suspicion of all those terms that constitute the work as an object, is the best way to enhance the chances of achieving a vital critical practice.

One way of affirming the singularity of literature, then, is to say that the literary occupies, in the practices and understandings of Western culture, the place of the other. (It is not alone in occupying this place, of course.) What I have undertaken to do in this book is no different from the many examples I have given within it of the project of converting alterity into familiarity, of accommodating the other as part of the same. My hope, however, is that in doing so I have registered and conveyed the significance of some of the tensions and slippages in our common understanding of literature and of art more generally, that my effort of accommodation has had an effect on the field itself. The same, as I have said many times, is no longer the same after the irruption of the other.

But more importantly, literature and the idea of literature, like the work of art that retains its singularity and otherness through many readings and many centuries precisely because it is not pure and enclosed but open to change, will not be domesticated by a book or a theory. For the literary too is impure, without fixed borders, liable to contamination and grafting, an event rather than an entity or a concept. My attempt to convey in the language of argument and description the essence of the literary has, of course, failed; but as an event communicated in the event of reading, this failure offers itself as testimony to the vitality and persistence of literature. To affirm responsibly the singularity of literature is both to analyze what appears, from the vantage point of the present, analyzable, and to acknowledge—as I have tried to do throughout this book—the necessary, even productive, limits of that enterprise.

Appendix: Debts and directions

Any attempt to identify one's intellectual debts in a project such as this one is, of course, bound to be inadequate: forty years of reading and listening lay down their traces in a dense palimpsest, much becoming buried beyond recall. But it may be useful to signal those of which I am most aware, partly to acknowledge, imperfectly but with gratitude, the degree to which the thoughts developed in this book originate in other minds and partly to offer readers some suggestions about where to turn for further reflections on the issues I have touched on. If anything in this book can be said to be an inventive contribution to the debate about the literary, it will not, as I have tried to argue, be because I have seized an absolutely new idea as it floated somewhere beyond everyone else's ken or performed a magical feat of creation *ex nihilo*; it will be because the multiple arguments and attitudes that I have imbibed have both provided a foundation for thinking and produced conflicts and fissures in my own thought out of which something new has emerged. That my own attempt to state a case for a certain understanding of the literary will have its blind spots, its tensions, its gaps, goes without saying; I am aware of some of them, but I am certain to be oblivious to the most important ones. The best that can be said about them is that they may be the places where readers will be spurred into their own acts of inventiveness.

The greatest debt of which I am conscious is to the thought of Jacques Derrida, primarily in the form of his published writings but also as manifested in numerous lectures, panel discussions, exchanges of letters, and private conversations. Derrida's work over the past thirty-five years constitutes the most significant, far-reaching, and inventive exploration of the importance of literature of our time.[1] It would be pointless to list all the published works by Derrida which I believe have influenced the writing of *The Singularity of Literature*; all I can do is single out a few which I believe are most directly related to the arguments I have presented here and which anyone interested in this topic should read. Some of these I collected in 1992 when I edited *Acts of Literature*, including ". . . That Dangerous Supplement . . ." from *Of Grammatology* (76–109), "The First Session," from *Dissemination* (127–80), "Before the Law" (183–220), "Ulysses Gramophone: Hear Say Yes in Joyce" (253–309), and, perhaps most important to me as a stimulus to further thought about literature and alterity, "Psyche: Invention of the Other" (311–43). The interview which I conducted with Derrida and published under the title "'This Strange Institution Called Literature'" (*Acts of Literature*, 33–75) has remained a rich resource. My thinking about ethics and responsibility has never been the same since I read *The Gift of Death*. Other works by Derrida that have particularly affected my sense of the literary and its relation to the ethical are *Altérités*, "Afterword," "Force of Law," "Che cos'è la poesia?," "Passions," *Aporias, Specters of Marx*, "La littérature au secret," and "A Self-Unsealing Poetic Text."

I will not attempt to list here the secondary works on Derrida, and on deconstruction more generally, that I have found valuable and that I would recommend to others. I would prefer just to list, in no particular order, a few names: Maud Ellmann, Robert Young, Geoffrey Bennington, David Carroll, Jonathan Culler, Thomas Keenan, Samuel Weber, Peggy Kamuf, Barbara Johnson, David Wills, Gayatri Chakravorty Spivak, Marian Hobson, J. Hillis Miller, Richard Rand, Rodolphe Gasché, Diane Elam, Jean-Michel Rabaté, and Nicholas Royle. It is my very good fortune that these names represent not just books and articles on my shelves—I indicate only a small selection of their work in the Bibliography—but also long-standing friendships from which I have benefited in manifold ways.

This book has also been influenced strongly by my reading of literary texts; again, I could mention dozens that might well have made a mark on my thinking, but one series of works stands out, both as instances of the literary and as compelling stagings of the questions I have raised (notably the question of responsibility to the other): the novels of J. M. Coetzee. Coetzee's non-fictional output has also been valuable to me, notably the interviews with David Attwell in *Doubling the Point* and the essay "Confession and Double Thoughts" in the same volume, as well as the hybrid work *Elizabeth Costello*. As I noted in the Preface, I had initially intended to write a book which combined discussions of Coetzee's writing with an argument about the literary, but those discussions are now to be found in a separate book, *J. M. Coetzee and the Ethics of Reading*. The works of James Joyce have also provided me with a stimulus to thought over a lengthy period; some of that history of engagement and influence is charted in *Joyce Effects*.

For the realization that an understanding of alterity is crucial to an understanding of the demands made by literary works upon us I am indebted to Emmanuel Levinas. Of all his work—and the years since his death have seen a flow of publications and translations—*Totality and Infinity* remains the book that for me most fully represents the challenge of his thought in the field of ethics. It needs to be supplemented, however, by his rethinking of the issues in *Otherwise than Being*, and in particular by his elaboration in that work of the distinction between the Saying and the Said. I should add that my appropriation of Levinas's thought is extremely selective, and also that his own discussions of literature and art do not go in the same direction as mine—see, for instance, his critical comments on "poetic activity" as a beguiling rhythm in need of disruption in *Totality and Infinity* (203). The extremes of his views on literature are to be found in "Reality and Its Shadow" (in which his view of art is, surprisingly, highly Platonic) and "Paul Celan: From Being to the Other" (in which he places a high valuation on one poet). My own argument comes closer to the suggestion made by Bernasconi and Critchley in their Introduction to *Re-Reading Levinas* that there might be a Levinasian hermeneutics which "would perhaps be defined by its readiness for re-reading because it would have no interest in distilling the content of a text into a 'said'" (xi).

Numerous commentaries on Levinas have been helpful to me in grappling with his troublesome work; let me mention only Derrida's "Violence and Metaphysics," which did so much to establish the importance of Levinas's work while delineating some of its problems, and his tribute after Levinas's death, *Adieu: to Emmanuel Levinas*; Jill Robbins's *Altered Reading*, which is the best study of the place of literature in Levinas's thought; and Michael Eskin's *Ethics and Dialogue*, which illuminatingly articulates Levinas's ethics with Bakhtin's dialogism in a discussion of poetic relations. The dialogic relation between reader and work, and between the cultural horizons by which each is shaped, is also a feature of Hans-Georg Gadamer's detailed elaboration of the historically conditioned character of understanding and of interpretation as event. In particular, this book bears traces of Gadamer's *Truth and Method* and of the essay "The Relevance of the Beautiful."

A writer who has been deeply engaged with the question of literature is Maurice Blanchot. Although Blanchot's prose is not the easiest to construe, I have often found it suggestively unsettling in its claims for and about the literary. The books I turn to most frequently are *The Space of Literature*, *The Infinite Conversation*, and *The Writing of the Disaster*. Also suggestive—above all in thinking about the event—have been many of the works of Jean-François Lyotard, notably *The Postmodern Condition*, *The Differend*, *The Postmodern Explained* and (with Jean-Loup Thébaud) *Just Gaming*. Lyotard has been lucky in his English-speaking commentators: both Geoffrey Bennington's *Lyotard: Writing the Event* and Bill Readings's *Introducing Lyotard* are much more than merely introductions.

A very different tradition of thought is represented by Theodor Adorno, but there can be no doubt that his *Aesthetic Theory* is among the most significant twentieth-century contributions to debates about artistic practice and response. I have found my struggles with it immensely rewarding, and its insistence on the historical situatedness of the production and reception of art has constantly informed my thinking. Also influential has been Adorno's championing of modern art as resistant to, while at the same time arising out of, the administrative and instrumental rationality that surrounds it. My encounter with J. M. Bernstein's *The Fate of Art* as I was completing this book was both clarifying and reassuring in its discussion of aesthetic modernity and its situating of Adorno in relation to Kant, Heidegger, and Derrida.

Alain Badiou should not, strictly speaking, figure in a list of debts as I did not come to know his work until after the arguments in this book were formulated. However, the numerous parallels I found when I did begin to read him—notably his short book *Ethics*—make it hard to leave him out, although our differences are finally greater than our agreements.

Echoes of many other accounts of the aesthetic, of art, and of literature will be evident in this book. Kant's *Critique of Judgment*, in detaching the idea of the beautiful (and the sublime) from the object and attributing it to the subject (without making it subjective in the limiting sense) set going the analysis of art of which this book is a late offshoot, and his account of genius is the source of much later thinking about the puzzle of artistic creativity, including mine. A number of commentators on Kant have been helpful; I would like to mention in particular Samuel Weber's lucid account of reflective judgment in "Ambivalence." In different ways, both Russian Formalism and Brechtian theory depict the importance of literature in terms of effects produced by a kind of self-estrangement arising from formal processes; both have had a significant influence on my argument, as has Tony Bennett's *Formalism and Marxism*, read a long time ago. I have often gone back to Heidegger remembering largely what I found rebarbative only to rediscover formulations that must have been silently effective in my thinking for a long time—notably his emphasis on art, and particularly poetry, in a number of late works, as well as his account of the "workly character of the work" and of creation and "createdness" in "The Origin of the Work of Art." No doubt my reading over many years of Wittgenstein (particularly of *Philosophical Investigations*), and many commentators on Wittgenstein, has had its influence too, especially in making me cautious about the search for closed definitions. A book I have found particularly valuable in articulating the common ground between the analytic and continental traditions of philosophy is Henry Staten's *Wittgenstein and Derrida*.

Many decades ago, Jean-Paul Sartre, in *What is Literature?*, raised the question of invention in reading. Roland Barthes has long been a source of pleasurable stimulation, making it difficult to single out works of particular importance for this book; perhaps the most relevant is *Camera Lucida*, with its problematic but suggestive distinction between *studium* and *punctum*.[2] Another Barthesian distinction, between *signifiance* (as process) and *signification* (as existent), long ago implanted the idea of literary meaning as event ("Theory of the Text," 37–8). Mikhail Bakhtin's emphasis in *Toward a Philosophy of the Act* on the "once-occurrent uniqueness or singularity" (13) of the act and the responsibility that is bound up with it struck a chord; Michel Foucault, too, helped clarify the status of the event in history, especially in the argument of *The Archaeology of Knowledge*. Paul de Man in a number of works challenged, irritated, invigorated; the work which perhaps made its mark most powerfully on my thinking is *The Resistance to Theory*. In *The Ethics of Reading* J. Hillis Miller pursues a de Manian argument that helped to stimulate my own consideration of the demands of the literary work. My sense of the pressures and exclusions of any given cultural formation, although largely derived from Derrida's account of *différance* and the trace, has also been sharpened by Fredric Jameson's analysis of the political dimension of such hidden tensions in *The Political Unconscious.*

A writer who has elaborated a theory of reading with some similarities to mine is Wolfgang Iser. In *The Implied Reader* and *The Act of Reading,* drawing on Roman Ingarden and John Dewey, Iser emphasizes the way in which the reading of a literary text—and in particular the activity stimulated by the lacunae in what the text presents—may cause us to suspend the habits that constitute us as subjects (see, in particular, *The Implied Reader,* 291, and *The Act of Reading,* 131–4). A historical focus on the changing significance of literary works in changing cultural contexts was provided by Hans Robert Jauss; see *Toward an Ethic of Reception.* Stanley Fish's early project of "affective stylistics" emphasized the eventness of linguistic meaning (see the essay "Literature in the Reader: Affective Stylistics"), and Fish's resistance, in a series of works, to any notion of absolute otherness as a motor for change helped me to articulate an opposing position. For a valuable discussion of the breakdown of a coherent subjectivity that, according to a variety of witnesses across the history of Western culture, marks the act-event of creation, see Timothy Clark, *The Theory of Inspiration.* I have also found Clark's *Derrida, Heidegger, Blanchot* very useful. A series of books and articles by Jean-Jacques Lecercle—*Philosophy through the Looking-Glass, The Violence of Language, The Philosophy of Nonsense,* and *Interpretation as Pragmatics*—have informed and stimulated me over the years, and Krzysztof Ziarek's account of the "force of art" (see his forthcoming book of that title) has developed along a path that intersects in interesting ways with my own.

After this book was complete, I returned to a work I had not read for many years, Louise M. Rosenblatt's *The Reader, the Text, the Poem,* and found much in her account of "transactional reading" that chimes with my argument for reading as performance. Two books appeared too late to form part of the writing of this one but reassured me that the issues I am confronting are of considerable contemporary importance, even though my approach and my conclusions are finally quite different. George Steiner's *Grammars of Creation* touches, sometimes in very similar terms, on a number of the puzzles about invention with which

I engage, and in Peter de Bolla's *Art Matters* I recognize an endeavor to articulate the importance of the experience of the artwork in its singularity and inventiveness that is in many ways parallel to mine.

Notes

1 Introductory

1 My chosen starting-point in *Peculiar Language*—the Renaissance—was to some extent arbitrary: it would have been possible to go as far back as Ancient Greece, where a similar argument could be developed in relation to terms of literary judgment indicating an appropriateness to the specific situation, such as *to prepon*, *metron*, and *kairos*. For a valuable discussion of these terms, see Ford, *The Origins of Criticism*, 12–22.

2 I use the adjective "Western" in this book simply as a disclaimer: I know too little of the traditions and cultures that are labeled "non-Western" to be able to say with confidence to what degree my arguments are applicable to any of them. I take this to be an empirical question, but one that I am not equipped to answer. Of course, the increasing domination exercised by historically Western ideas around the globe, in the wake of increasing economic domination, means that their applicability is likely to grow—a fact that I am not in any way intending to celebrate.

3 An indication of the degree to which these questions have been ignored in some arenas of philosophical debate is provided by the indexes to two recently published volumes (of over 500 and 800 pages respectively, the *Routledge Companion to Aesthetics*, edited by Gaut and Lopes, and the *Oxford Handbook of Aesthetics*, edited by Levinson. These reference books cover a vast range of topics, yet the reader will search in vain for entries for "alterity," "invention," "otherness," and "singularity," and only one—in the Routledge volume—for "innovation." This last recommends a book whose reductiveness is unashamedly advertised in its title, Colin Martindale's *The Clockwork Muse: The Predictability of Artistic Change*. Martindale's study has the virtue of acknowledging the centrality of innovation to the history of Western art, but seeks to explain this in terms of a simple model of "habituation." That artworks may continue to possess

what Martindale terms "arousal potential" centuries after their creation is not a problem he addresses.

4 One indication of this recurrent difficulty is the long history of attempts to define an unfathomable, supplementary *je ne sais quoi* that distinguishes literary from non-literary uses of language. I discuss some significant moments in this history in *Peculiar Language*.

5 J. M. Coetzee, *Disgrace*, 3.

6 My comments should not be construed as an attack on "professionalism" of the kind much in evidence in recent years; that concept is more complex and historically situated than is implied in such denunciations, as Bruce Robbins has shown in *Secular Vocations*.

7 Marxist criticism and feminist criticism, for example, are by definition instrumentalist to some degree: literary works are read in the light of a pre-existing set of assumptions, values, and goals that derive from the social and political realm (understood as clearly distinguishable from the "aesthetic" realm). One should not, however, overlook the many examples of such criticism which respond to the singularity of the literary works they read, in addition to (and in the best instances, as part of) their political instrumentality. Nor should one overlook the fact that *every* reading, instrumental or not, involves consciously and unconsciously held assumptions, values, and goals. I should also make it clear that I am not talking about historical studies of the *contexts* within which particular literary works were produced and first received; such studies often contribute valuably to the reading of the works in question.

8 Terry Eagleton's *Ideology of the Aesthetic* relies on this understanding of the tradition, and offers discussions of many of its major proponents.

9 The label "New Criticism" is applied to a wide array of individual critical projects, which, it is interesting to note, frequently had a strong instrumental element. This purpose was usually couched in humanist ethical terms, though there were also psychologically oriented versions like that of I. A. Richards, religiously oriented versions like that of C. S. Lewis, and politically oriented versions like that of the early Raymond Williams.

10 The cultural analyst who has done most to demystify the aesthetic in this way is Pierre Bourdieu; see, for example, *Distinction* and *The Rules of Art*.

11 See Jay Bernstein, *The Fate of Art*, 3–4. Bernstein identifies Kant's Third Critique as the source of the modern separation between aesthetics and truth, notwithstanding Kant's own goal of bridging these domains. I should add that Bernstein yokes "goodness" with "truth" in this discussion, though it seems to me less clear that modern notions of the autonomy of the aesthetic have set all ethical claims aside.

2 Creation and the other

1 The notion of creation is sometimes avoided by theorists of the aesthetic, not least because of its theological origins. It has long been an object of suspicion among Marxist theorists, some of whom prefer to understand art purely in terms of production. (For a concise example, see Pierre Macherey's chapter "Creation and Production" in his *Theory of Literary Production*, 66–8.) But there has been wide recognition that conditions of production, however important, cannot exhaustively explain the coming-into-being of the hitherto unexampled; see, for instance, the chapter entitled "Creative Practice" in Raymond Williams, *Marxism and Literature*, 206–12.

2 All acts of creation (including the one I am engaged in here) are, of course, conditioned by their historical circumstances. The apparently Cartesian method of my investigation should not be taken to imply a claim that transhistorical and transcultural experiences are possible.

3 A parallel distinction is the one often made between the methodology and aims of linguistics—the investigation of the grammatical system of a language, for instance, or of the properties shared by all grammatical systems—and the methodology and aims of psycholinguistics—the study of the events that occur in the brain when a sentence is uttered, for instance, or the capacity humans have for remembering word meanings.

4 *Elizabeth Costello*, 27.

5 This notion of "cultural field" is much too simple. I will return to it, and to the question of the individual's relation to the cultural context within which he or she is situated, in the following section.

6 The process I describe here in a somewhat impressionistic manner has been depicted more systematically (if perhaps more simplistically) in the terms provided by the approach to human knowledge known as "schema theory," an approach derived ultimately from Kant but developed in cognitive psychology and studies of artificial intelligence before being applied to discourse analysis and accounts of literature. See, in particular, Guy Cook's argument, in *Discourse and Literature*, that it is characteristic of literature to disrupt the reader's schemata, producing what he calls "schema refreshment" (or cognitive change) at one or more of three levels: content, literary structure, and language. What makes Cook's work more valuable in discussions of art than other versions of schema theory which put all their emphasis on the cognitive dimension is his claim that it is by means of deviation at one or more of these levels that the disruption occurs. He thus includes the formal properties of the literary work in his analysis, though it has to be said that the notion of deviation and the connections between levels remain problematic areas in his account.

7 Creation and its relation to the human context in which it occurs has sometimes been described in rather different terms derived from the later Wittgenstein: "forms of life" instead of "culture," and "language games" for the various and often contradictory and open-ended linguistic systems which shape our existences; see, for example, Morris Weitz, "The Role of Theory in Aesthetics," and Matthew Rampley, "Creativity." Although the emphasis in such arguments on open-endedness and incommensurability is valuable, and although Wittgenstein's discussions of "family resemblances" and "following a rule" allow for less prescriptive accounts of art than do many other philosophical systems, they do not address the issues in which I am most interested here.

8 I am echoing the title of a demanding and suggestive essay by Jacques Derrida: "Psyche: Invention of the Other."

9 This familiar point is clearly articulated by Kant in his discussion of genius: "If an author owes a product to his genius, he himself does not know how he came by the ideas for it; nor is it in his power to devise such products at his pleasure, or by following a plan" (*Critique of Judgment*, 175 [Ak. 308]).

10 Jacques Derrida, "'Entre le corps écrivant,'" 70.

11 Cited by John Lahr, "Making It Real," 207.

12 The "double determination" of the created work was acknowledged as early as Homeric epic; for instance, the singer Demodocus is described, in conscious paradox, as follows: "A god has granted him above all others the gift of song, / To delight us with whatever his heart prompts him to sing" (*Odyssey*, 8.44–5). In the twentieth century, Adorno encapsulated this contradiction in a typical aphorism: "By exigency, the new must be something willed; as what is other, however, it could not be what was willed" (*Aesthetic Theory*, 22).

13 Peter Kivy, in *The Possessor and the Possessed*, examines these two models of creation, proceeding from two contrasting conceptions of genius which he terms the Platonic (from the theory presented in the *Ion*) and the Longinian. Kivy does not, however, see them as necessarily co-implicated.

14 Alain Badiou speaks of the "void" or the "not-known" of a situation which the creative event names (*Ethics*, 68–9); his is a more rigid understanding of the requirements for creativity (the void is said to lie "at the heart of every situation, as the foundation of its being"), but has some affinities with mine.

15 "Every scientist must occasionally turn around and ask not merely, 'How can I solve this problem?' but, 'Now that I have come to a result, what problem have I solved?'" (Wiener, *Invention*, 22).

16 I shall sometimes use the term "act-event" to refer to the creative process in its various forms, but when I use either "event" or "act" alone for this purpose, it may be taken to mean *both* event and act—and hence neither

event nor act in their usual senses. The many different philosophical uses of the notion of the event—it plays an important part in the thinking of, among others, Heidegger, Derrida, Lyotard, Deleuze, and Badiou—make it a particularly problematic term to use. In some respects, the term "happening" would be more suitable, since it does not carry with it the same amount of philosophical baggage and emphasizes the verbal character of what is at stake; it would be an awkward substitution, however, and might imply the complete irrelevance of the philosophical discourses I have mentioned, which would be equally misleading.

17 A related term, with a more philosophical pedigree, is *aporia*—see, for instance, Derrida, *Aporias*, and Richard Beardsworth, *Derrida and the Political*, both *passim*. Foucault's "problematization" is another kindred term (though Foucault would probably have contested the connection with Derrida); see "Polemics, Politics, and Problematizations."

18 I use "accommodate" for this process, since it suggests that the other is converted to the same not by being itself transformed but by transforming the culture that receives it. An alternative might be "assimilate"—which shares an Indo-European root with "same"—but this has the disadvantage of implying the transformation of the other within an unchanging culture.

19 *Tout autre est tout autre* is the pregnant motto Derrida coins in *The Gift of Death* (68 and *passim*): every other is completely other.

20 Badiou refers to the event of the "coming-to-be of that which is not yet" (*Ethics*, 27) and its "incalculable novelty" (32), noting that it "is heterogeneous to the instituted knowledges of the situation" (43), and yet he distances himself from all discourses of the "other" (18–29), perhaps partly to disguise his closeness to some of them.

21 Derrida questions Levinas's notion of the "infinitely other" in "Violence and Metaphysics," insisting on the relationality implicit in the idea of the other: "The infinitely other," he imagines Parmenides arguing, "can be what it is only if it is other, that is, other *than*. *Other than* must be *other than* myself. Henceforth, it is no longer absolved of a relation to an ego. Therefore, it is no longer infinitely, absolutely other." Derrida endorses this imagined argument, asserting that "the other cannot be absolutely exterior to the same without ceasing to be other" (126).

22 Here I depart significantly from Levinas, who is the source of much of my thinking on the subject of the other; for Levinas, the ultimate other is God, an absolute, unconditioned, wholly transcendent Other. However, it is testimony to the fertility of his elaboration of an ethics of alterity that it has been possible for others—the most important example being Derrida—to develop it without accepting its theological dimension.

23 Frequently, the oppression of a culture or people is described in terms of their categorization as "other" (hence the verb "to other"). In such a relation, there is no creativity, no response to alterity and singularity; as

Derrida notes, "Racism is also an invention of the other, but in order to exclude it and tighten the circle of the same" ("Psyche," 336 n.17).

24 These phrases from the tradition of the novel (George Eliot) and of phenomenology suggest the generalizing power of these moral discourses; I do not wish to suggest, however, that they do not also allow for the response to the singularity of the other I am discussing here.

25 Hence the appropriateness of the term "hospitality" in this context. Hospitality toward the other—whether a person, a group, or a not-yet-formulated thought or formal possibility—implies a willingness not just to accept the other into one's own domain, but to change that domain, perhaps radically, in order to make the other welcome. See Derrida and Dufourmantelle, *Of Hospitality*, and Derrida, "Hostipitality."

26 Similarly, I. A. Richards, advancing a theory of art as communication, has to deal with the fact that "the artist is not as a rule consciously concerned with communication, but with getting the work, the poem or play or statue or painting or whatever it is, 'right,' apparently regardless of its communicative efficacy" (*Principles of Literary Criticism*, 18).

3 Originality and invention

1 The concept of originality has a long pedigree in literary studies, often appearing in alliance with "genius" and in opposition to "imitation"; though it clearly owes much to Longinus' *On the Sublime*, its first full-dress appearance on the theoretical stage was in Edward Young's *Conjectures on Original Composition* of 1759.

2 For an account of the influences upon Kant's theory of originality, including Young (whose essay was introduced to Kant by J. G. Hamann), see Martin Gammon, "'Exemplary Originality': Kant on Genius and Imitation." Young, for whom the word "original" would have more strongly suggested its cognate "origin" than it does for us, says of original writers that they "extend the Republic of Letters, and add a new province to its dominion" (*Conjectures*, 10).

3 *Critique of Judgment*, 175, 186–7 (Ak. 307–8, 318).

4 As Adorno puts it, referring to what he calls the "encompassing norms" of a period and place: "There has probably scarcely ever been a work that was important in any regard that did not, by virtue of its own form, mediate these norms and thus virtually transform them" (*Aesthetic Theory*, 334). (That "in any regard" is perhaps an exaggeration, as unoriginal works may still be important in some respects, if not strictly as works of art.) Coetzee offers a counter-example in the figure of Joseph in *Elizabeth Costello* (134–41): a Zulu sculptor employed at a mission station in Natal, he carves the same derivative image of the crucifixion over and over again. To

Elizabeth this absence of any desire to innovate is a denial of art, although to her sister Blanche it marks the triumph of the Christian message over the failed legacy of the classical tradition.

5   Illuminating examples of the study of these formal transformations are, in the visual arts, E. H. Gombrich, *Art and Illusion*, and, in music, Charles Rosen, *The Classical Style* and *Schoenberg*.

6   Contemporary works, of course, require no historical knowledge for an appreciation of their originality (or lack of it), though they do rely on the receiver's cultural awareness. We shall return in due course to the special category of contemporary art; see p. 52.

7   Derrida's discussion of "invention" in "Psyche" is the best account of the word's knot of meanings. In Lyotard's vocabulary the closest term is "paralogy" or "paralogism," which denotes a practice that differs from "innovation" in the fact that it invents new rules (*The Postmodern Condition*, 43, 61; see also Bill Readings, *Introducing Lyotard*, 72–4). (I should add that my use of "innovation" is wider in its application than Lyotard's.)

8   George Steiner devotes several pages of *Grammars of Creation* (89–93, and *passim*) to the distinction between "invention" and "creation," though he also comments that "the entire distinction is suspect." My way of delineating the distinction trades on only one of the many differences in connotation.

9   We sometimes use the word "creation" in a sense close to "invention," as when we refer to the new creation of a fashion designer or a chef: here the individual concerned has probably not made any physical entity, but has brought into existence a design or a recipe that others can both emulate and use as a springboard for further creation. In this book, however, I am using "creation" in the narrower sense.

10   An invention can recur several times in different cultures and at different historical points; one example is the abacus (see Wiener, *Invention*, 12). Even more striking, perhaps, is the frequency with which an invention appears at roughly the same time in different countries at a similar stage of technological development—giving rise to interminable arguments about who really invented x.

11   F. R. Leavis, *Revaluation*, 18.

12   For Pound, too, "Literature is news that STAYS news" (*ABC of Reading*, 29).

13   Kant's somewhat puzzling refusal to ascribe genius to great scientific minds (*Critique of Judgment* 176–7; Ak. 308–9) may be an indirect reflection of this difference. He contrasts the possibility of tracking Newton's arguments by diligent study with the impossibility of retracing the creative processes of Homer or Wieland, a contrast which, it seems to me, is related to that between the historical distance of original philosophical work and the ever-present inventiveness of art.

14 In discussing the experience of a work of art that seems to speak directly across the ages—his example is Bach's *Well-tempered Clavier*—Coetzee argues that the historical and material basis of such a response does not invalidate it; on the contrary, it is what make trans-temporal aesthetic experience possible. See "What is a Classic?"

15 The evidence for Surrey's originality is not wholly compelling, but that does not affect the argument here.

16 There may be a case for claiming that the canons of art change in accordance with the principle proposed by Thomas Kuhn for the sciences in *The Structure of Scientific Revolutions*: it becomes more and more difficult for creative artists to maintain a given mode as its limitations are increasingly exposed and its responses to the demands of a changing world are more and more strained, until an individual—a Caravaggio or a Defoe—finds a way of re-articulating their materials that allows the other to come into being, and a new phase is begun. This is not a claim I would press, since the history of artistic production seems to follow more varied patterns than a Kuhnian model would allow, but it does provide a useful way of conceptualizing some of the large-scale shifts in cultural history.

17 The infrequency of such matching of the contexts of production and reception, whether across time or across space, is not simply to be regretted; my argument is that the experience of artistic inventiveness is often made possible by cultural *differences*, working in conjunction with cultural overlappings.

18 As Lionel Trilling puts it in "The Sense of the Past": "In the existence of every work of literature of the past, its historicity, its *pastness*, is a factor of great importance. . . . It is a part of the *given* of the work, which we cannot help but respond to" (184–5).

19 For a sprightlier exposition of this point than Eliot's, see Borges's essay, "Kafka's Precursors" (*Labyrinths*, 199–201).

4 Inventive language and the literary event

1 This, at least, is philosophy's predominant self-conception. The unavoidability of mediation via language, and the effects of this on the philosophical project, have been the theme of much philosophical and para-philosophical writing, especially since the middle of the twentieth century.

2 Saussure's distinction between *langue* and *parole* is one well-known attempt to deal with this fact (*Course in General Linguistics*, 9–15). Saussure's terms—unlike Chomsky's reinterpretation of them under the names "competence" and "performance"—highlight the different *status* of the two modes of existence of the sign, as object (a somewhat strange

psychological object that is at once individual and social) and as event. This difference in status—which is less like contrasting apples with oranges than like contrasting apples with the picking of apples—has led to many misunderstandings and misapplications of the distinction; see my discussion in "The Linguistic Model and Its Application," 58–84.

3 Note that the sense of purposiveness I am elaborating here is to be distinguished from that which Kant uses in his attempt to account for the operation of reflective (aesthetic) judgment. What Kant is responding to is the apparent lawfulness of nature which makes subjective cognition possible (hence "purposiveness without purposes"); my concern is with the attributed purposiveness whereby the subject understands an empirical object as a human artifact. See "Authoredness" in Chapter 7 below.

4 I am limiting this discussion to verbal texts, but much of it would be applicable, *mutatis mutandis*, to nonverbal or only partly verbal texts that exist in a temporal medium like film, dance, and the many varieties of music. A movie or a ballet is even more obviously an event than a novel, partly because the inscribed "text" is clearly a less fully realized version than the performance. To extend the argument to non-temporal texts, like photography and painting, would require some recasting of its terms, but I believe it would still be essentially valid.

5 "The Task of the Translator," in *Illuminations*, 70. Aristotle might be thought to have set the discussion of literature going on the wrong track by emphasizing, in the *Poetics*, the pleasure offered by the imitative arts to those who learn about the world from them. This remains a minor element in his account, however; much more significant is his recognition that tragedies, even when read, are events involving reversals and the arousing of pity and fear. See Ford, *The Origins of Criticism*, 266–70.

6 Coetzee dramatizes this uncertainty and risk in *The Master of Petersburg*; see Derek Attridge, *J. M. Coetzee and the Ethics of Reading*, Chapter 5.

7 For a brief account of the history of the term, see the entry under "Literature" in Raymond Williams, *Keywords*.

5 Singularity

1 For instance, the term is sometimes used to mean an individual completely without relations outside itself (a meaning recently developed in Peter Hallward's *Absolutely Postcolonial*); as will become clear, this sense has very little to do with mine.

2 The word itself took on the meaning of a self-advertising refusal to conform to norms in the late sixteenth century, although according to the *OED*, this meaning ceased to be common after 1700.

3 William Blake, *Songs of Innocence and Experience* (1794), Plate 39.

4 See Borges, "Pierre Menard, Author of the *Quixote*," in *Labyrinths* (36–44).

5 A traditional metrical analysis in terms of "feet" would give the erroneous impression that the poem is rhythmically complex, either "anapaestic dimeter" with many "iambic substitutions" or "iambic dimeter" with many "anapaestic substitutions." (In fact, by such an analysis, there are eight "anapaests" and eight "iambs," so it is impossible to say what the "basic" meter is.) Its simple rhythmic drive is brought out by analyzing it in terms of beats and offbeats; see Attridge, *The Rhythms of English Poetry*, Chapter 4, and *Poetic Rhythm: An Introduction*, Chapters 3 and 4.

6 The terms used in this description of phrasal movement are taken from Chapter 8 of my *Poetic Rhythm*.

7 T. S. Eliot, "Milton I."

6   Reading and responding

1 In *What is Literature?* Sartre formulates a view of the literary work that has some similarities with this account. If his view of reading makes it a "re-invention," he states, "such a re-invention would be as new and as original an act as the first invention" (30–1). For Sartre, this structure of invention answered by invention is peculiar to the literary field; I am arguing that it occurs much more widely.

2 Derrida uses the trope of signature and counter-signature to describe this process; see, for example, "'This Strange Institution Called Literature," 66–70. I discuss the signature further in Chapter 8.

3 These rules are not inherent in the object, nor do they necessarily correspond to anything in the creative process; they are what constitute the object as meaningful *in a given cultural context*. There is no guarantee that they will remain unchanged in other temporal or geographical contexts. (Although they make imitation possible, an exact imitation at a particular time may come to seem inexact in a different context.) It is this qualification that is frequently ignored by critics in what I earlier called the aesthetic tradition. Helen Vendler is a good example: "The aim of an aesthetic criticism is to *describe* the art work in such a way that it cannot be confused with any other art work (not an easy task), and to *infer* from its elements the aesthetic that might generate this unique configuration" (*The Music of What Happens*, 2).

4 We should note that explanation is more than description, though the latter may be an important part of explanation. To engage in the process of "accurate description" is to make decisions about which of the myriad features of the work merit description—the use of archaic words? the use of polysyllabic words? the use of five-letter words? the typeface? the color of the ink? The list is potentially endless, and the choices made in any

description will reflect a prior theory of what is relevant to an explanation of the work's meaningfulness and power.

5 See Russell and Winterbottom, *Ancient Literary Criticism*, 87, 103, 116, 134.

6 Peter de Bolla's *Art Matters* has much of value to say about encounters with inventive and singular artworks, but his account differs from mine in being primarily concerned with psychological experience. His lengthy and often strenuous descriptions of his experience of three specific works in different modes illustrate both the strengths and weaknesses of such an approach.

7 This is not to suggest that a responsible reading is impossible without a background of wide reading and intense scholarly effort: a reader who does not command this kind of knowledge and training may nevertheless become so closely engaged with a work as to intuit many of its relevant contextual features and apprehend its significant elements. Although there is bound to be a greater element of chance in such a response, it is important to acknowledge that no amount of scholarly and critical labor could ever be deemed "enough" and that there is therefore always some degree of contingency in the exercise.

8 See I. A. Richards, *Principles of Literary Criticism*, 158–9, and *Practical Criticism*, 240–54.

9 It is sometimes argued that the beautiful object is characterized by the arousal of the desire to reduplicate itself in words or other media; see, for example, Elaine Scarry, *On Beauty and Being Just*. However, this response is far from universal, and is probably connected to certain kinds of education and training. We should not confuse, as Scarry does, the desire to reduplicate the art-object with the desire to preserve or sustain its singularity and inventiveness, a topic treated in Chapter 10 below.

7 Performance

1 This is not a peculiarity of the literary artwork, or even the temporally linear artwork; we can be said to "perform" paintings, buildings, sculpture, installations, and photographs when we respond to them as art. Adorno has a similar sense of a full response to artworks: "Understanding specific artworks . . . requires an objective experiential reenactment from within in the same sense in which the interpretation of a musical work means its faithful performance" (*Aesthetic Theory*, 121).

2 The notion of "aboutness," proposed by Arthur C. Danto in *The Transfiguration of the Commonplace* as an essential ingredient of the aesthetic work, is related to this quality of self-distance. However, Danto speaks of it as an attribute rather than an event.

3   I develop this argument in "Against Allegory," Chapter 2 of *J. M. Coetzee and the Ethics of Reading*.

4   In some artworks, notably film, it is impossible to separate the "work" and the "performance"; my concern here is with works that have a verbal existence more autonomous than that of a film-script.

5   Frank Lentricchia and Andrew Dubois, eds, *Close Reading*.

6   George Herbert, "Easter" (*The Temple*, 1633). As Tobin notes in his edition of Herbert's poetry, the two distinct parts of what he prints as one poem are often printed as two, "Easter (1)" and "Easter (2)," in which case the cited lines form the first stanza of the second poem (341).

7   A first and a second reading, even if one immediately follows the other, are likely to be significantly different, as we saw above (p. 88).

8   My emphasis on presupposed purposiveness as distinct from the historical intentions the work may embody and to the ascertainable facts about its creation should not be taken to imply an attempt to delegitimize the study of these matters. The attempt to do full justice to a work may well include just this kind of biographical and historical activity, even though the *effect* of such activity upon reading—creative reading—can never be predicted. The accumulation of facts may open readings as much as it may close them, whatever the motives of the biographer or historian.

9   Both Bakhtin's and Levinas's understanding of discourse depends on some such presupposition. For a suggestive discussion of this shared premise, and of its ethical implications, see Michael Eskin, *Ethics and Dialogue*. Heidegger's emphasis on "createdness" as "part of the created work" has some affinities with what I am arguing, though his concern is with the effect of remarkable artistic achievements rather than art *per se* ("The Origin of the Work of Art," 64). Note that authoredness differs from the concept of an "implied author": The latter is one of many verbal effects dependent on a prior assumption of authoredness.

10 My reference to the "human" reflects the dominant current conception of the literary; it is important to leave open, however, the possibility that this is a limit that future inventiveness, perhaps taking advantage of developments in technology, will breach. There can be no intrinsic restriction on the form which the other will take, and thus no pre-specification of its humanness; if there were, it would already be compromised, and not wholly other. The experience of authoredness may at some future date not be limited to the human domain, and literature may already be in the process of undermining the human/non-human distinction.

11 What the author "meant" by doing so is not the issue; it is perfectly possible to take pleasure in an irresolvable uncertainty about whether certain effects were intended or not (see Attridge, *Joyce Effects*, 121–5).

12 Recent work in the field of genetic criticism, however, has made it possible

to engage more fully with texts that have not reached a finalized form. See, for example, *Genesis*, the journal of the Parisian group ITEM.

13 Edward W. Said, *Musical Elaborations*, 89, and Antony Sher, *Beside Myself: An Autobiography*, 322. (Oddly, when Said extends this idea to literature he applies it to critical essays rather than to performances of literary works.)

14 One of the most interesting discussions of what it is to read a literary work is Blanchot's account in *The Space of Literature*—see especially Section VI, "Communication and the Work." Blanchot discusses the work's genesis, and asserts that

> reading draws whoever reads the work into the remembrance of that profound genesis. Not that the reader necessarily perceives afresh the manner in which the work was produced—not that he is in attendance at the real experience of its creation. But he partakes of the work as the unfolding of something in the making. (202)

8 Form, meaning, context

1 Post-structuralist literary criticism often discusses formal aspects by means of the term "signifier," countering notions of organic form by insisting on the autonomy of the material forms of language. Unfortunately, such talk hardly escapes the Aristotelian straitjacket; it further reifies form, ignoring Saussure's insistence on the inseparability of signifier and signified, and failing to appreciate the way in which meaning is always implicit in anything that can be called a signifier as distinct from a non-signifying material entity. (By the same token, the signified in Saussurean linguistics is never detachable from the signifier—a point whose significance Derrida has developed at length.)

2 See, in particular, "Signature Event Context" and "Signsponge."

3 Though I have used "act" in discussing the signature, we should not lose sight of the eventness of the procedure: the difference between signing and writing my name is that the former involves a certain passivity as I let habit and muscular memory take over the pen. Similarly, recognizing a signature is something that happens to me as much as something I do.

4 Recent developments in the technology of signature recognition bring out the degree to which a signature is an act-event of producing a form: for instance, a customer proffering a credit card may be asked to sign on a machine that detects whether the tracing motions whereby the form is produced correspond to those which brought the master-signature into existence. A would-be forger may produce a recognizable signature, but by means of an unrecognizable act.

5 Levinas, in calling for an attention to the Saying rather than the Said on which philosophy concentrates, is pointing to a similar distinction (although for different, if not unrelated, reasons). See *Otherwise than Being, passim.*

6 Robert Royston, ed., *Black Poets in South Africa*, 24. Some twenty-five years late, I wish to thank Colin Gardner for introducing Serote's poetry to me.

7 In my discussion of the poem, I am taking, with no justification, my own response as typical. I believe this to be a harmless strategy; it is certainly one for which there are many precedents. My hope would be, of course, that my commentary will have a positive effect on readers who, on their first engagement with the poem, do not experience the intensity that I do.

8 "Black like me" is the last line of Hughes's "Dream Variations."

9 "Baas" is used of strangers as well as known white masters; an equivalent term in the other direction would be "boy" or "John." Although considered historically the poem reflects the apartheid state of the 1970s, the situation could easily arise today, or could have arisen fifty years earlier.

10 Since J. L. Austin's introduction of the term "performative" into the analysis of language use in *How to Do Things with Words*, it has been put to a remarkable variety of uses, some of them entirely justified, others less so. Although one could adduce similarities between the sense in which I am using "performance" and Austin's account of performative utterances, I do not wish to press the connection. (For a valuable attempt to make such a link, see Andrew Parker and Eve Sedgwick, eds, *Performativity and Performance*.) Derrida argues for the necessity of going beyond the performative in welcoming the other ("The University without Condition," 234).

11 See Attridge, "Le texte comme autre: la forme sans formalisme."

9 Responsibility and ethics

1 Coetzee is an exception: "The *feel* of writing fiction is one of freedom, of irresponsibility, or better, of responsibility toward something that has not yet emerged, that lies somewhere at the end of the road" (*Doubling the Point*, 246).

2 For a discussion of the importance of trust in the ethical relation, see Attridge, *J. M. Coetzee and the Ethics of Reading*, Chapter 4.

3 In *What is Literature?*, Sartre emphasizes the importance of generosity on the part of the reader, linking generosity to freedom (36–9).

4 Such an outcome would be likely to lead to the retrospective reinterpretation of the event as uninventive, since it would not give rise to further invention, but rather to a closing down of possibilities. The flourishing of

Nazism may be a historical example: most of those to whom it appealed as an apparently inventive event could not have foreseen the Final Solution. Badiou interestingly cites Nazism as an example of a "simulacrum" of a truth, arising from an event that was "formally indistinguishable" from a genuine event in his sense (and thus deceiving Heidegger, among others) (*Ethics*, 72–7).

5 Although "morality" is defined in many ways, it is often associated with a more knowable and codifiable set of norms than ethics. For a discussion of the distinction between ethics and morality which adverts to other understandings of these concepts, see Geoffrey Galt Harpham, *Getting It Right*, 49–56. Dwight Furrow provides a cogent account of the various movements in recent ethical philosophy that have challenged generalizing theories; see *Against Theory*.

6 One way of talking about the other is as *the law*, understood as an obligation which is never manifested as such, but only in specific, and alterable, laws, in stories about the law, etc. A powerful representation of the law as other is Kafka's fable "Before the Law"; and see Derrida's essay of the same name, which reprints the fable in its entirety (*Acts of Literature*, 183–220).

7 There is a long and worthy tradition of literary analysis and evaluation in terms of its value as—to use the title of an essay by Kenneth Burke—"equipment for living"; the most distinguished member of this tradition today is Martha C. Nussbaum (see, for example, *Love's Knowledge*). Many writers of literary works have possessed unusual wisdom about the choices that face individuals and societies (a wisdom that sometimes emerged only in their literary productions), and there is much to be gained from experiencing their works—as there is from experiencing the concrete human situations represented in the writings of essayists, moralists, historians, biographers, philosophers, and theologians. This value is not, however, a distinctive property of literature.

8 Here I am echoing Derrida's short essay, "Che cos'è la poesia?"

9 This arbitrary hailing by the other can be contrasted with Louis Althusser's motivated interpellation by an ideology—a scheme which might be a good model for a relation to a text that does *not* involve responsibility (see "Ideology and Ideological State Apparatuses").

10   An everyday impossibility

1 George Steiner, *Grammars of Creation*, 122.

2 We can never know exactly what cultural conditions made possible this or that artistic work or generic revolution, but an understanding of the process of invention can lead to detailed and illuminating historical study of the emergence of new forms. One example is Michael McKeon's study

of the origins of the English novel, which—although it uses different terminology from mine—charts the cultural tensions and contradictions in English culture which made the invention of the novel possible (and perhaps necessary) (*The Origins of the English Novel, 1600–1740*).

Appendix: Debts and directions

1 Nothing could be further from the truth than the notion, promulgated not only by journalists but also by some well-known literary critics who ought to know better, that Derrida's work constitutes an attack on literature.

2 Some of the connections between this book and the present argument will be evident in my essay "Roland Barthes's Obtuse, Sharp Meaning and the Responsibilities of Criticism."

Bibliography

Adorno, Theodor W. *Aesthetic Theory.* Ed. Gretel Adorno and Rolf Tiedemann. Trans. Robert Hullot-Kentor. Minneapolis, Minn.: University of Minnesota Press, 1997.

Althusser, Louis. "Ideology and Ideological State Apparatuses: Notes toward an Investigation." *Lenin and Philosophy and Other Essays.* Trans. Ben Brewster. New York: Monthly Review Press, 1971, pp. 127–86.

Aristotle. *Poetics. Ancient Literary Criticism.* Ed. D. A. Russell and M. Winterbottom. Oxford: Oxford University Press, 1971, pp. 85–132.

Attridge, Derek. "Deconstruction and Fiction." *Deconstructions: A User's Guide.* Ed. Nicholas Royle. Basingstoke: Palgrave, 2000, pp. 105–18.

——. "Innovation, Literature, Ethics: Relating to the Other." *PMLA* 114 (1999): 20–31.

——. *J. M. Coetzee and the Ethics of Reading: Literature in the Event.* Chicago: University of Chicago Press, and Pietermaritzburg: University of Natal Press, 2004.

——. *Joyce Effects: On Language, Theory, and History.* Cambridge: Cambridge University Press, 2000.

——. "The Linguistic Model and Its Application." *The Cambridge History of Literary Criticism,* vol. 8: *From Formalism to Poststructuralism.* Ed. Raman Selden. Cambridge: Cambridge University Press, 1995, pp. 58–84.

——. *Peculiar Language: Literature as Difference from the Renaissance to James Joyce.* 1988. Reissue, London: Routledge, 2004.

——. *Poetic Rhythm: An Introduction.* Cambridge: Cambridge University Press, 1995.

——. *The Rhythms of English Poetry.* London: Longman, 1982.

——. "Roland Barthes's Obtuse, Sharp Meaning and the Responsibilities of Criticism." *Writing the Image after Roland Barthes.* Ed. Jean-Michel Rabaté. Philadelphia, Pa.: University of Pennsylvania Press, 1997, pp. 77–89.

——. "Le texte comme autre: la forme sans formalisme." *Le Passage des frontières: Autour du travail de Jacques Derrida*. Ed. Marie-Louise Mallet. Paris: Galilée, 1994, pp. 53–5.

Austin, J. L. *How to Do Things with Words*. 2nd edn. Oxford: Oxford University Press, 1975.

Badiou, Alain. *Ethics: An Essay on the Understanding of Evil*. Trans. Peter Hallward. London: Verso, 2001.

——. *L'Etre et l'événement*. Paris: Seuil, 1988.

Bakhtin, Mikhail. *Toward a Philosophy of the Act*. Ed. Vadim Liapanov and Michael Holquist. Trans. Vadim Liapanov. Austin, Tex.: University of Texas Press, 1993.

Barthes, Roland. *Camera Lucida: Reflections on Photography*. Trans. Richard Howard. New York: Hill & Wang, 1981.

——. "Theory of the Text." *Untying the Text: A Post-Structuralist Reader*. Ed. Robert Young. London: Routledge, 1981, pp. 31–47.

Beardsworth, Richard. *Derrida and the Political*. London: Routledge, 1996.

Benjamin, Walter. *Illuminations*. Ed. Hannah Arendt. Trans. Harry Zohn. London: Collins/Fontana, 1973, pp. 69–82.

Bennett, Tony. *Formalism and Marxism*. London: Methuen, 1979.

Bennington, Geoffrey. *Interrupting Derrida*. London: Routledge, 2000.

——. *Legislations: The Politics of Deconstruction*. London: Verso, 1994.

——. *Lyotard: Writing the Event*. New York: Columbia University Press, 1988.

Bernasconi, Robert, and Simon Critchley, eds. *Re-Reading Levinas*. Bloomington, Ind.: Indiana University Press, 1991.

Bernstein, J. M. *The Fate of Art: Aesthetic Alienation from Kant to Derrida and Adorno*. University Park, Pa.: Pennsylvania State University Press, 1992.

Blanchot, Maurice. *The Infinite Conversation*. Trans. Susan Hanson. Minneapolis, Minn.: University of Minnesota Press, 1993.

——. *The Space of Literature*. Trans. Ann Smock. Lincoln, Nebr.: University of Nebraska Press, 1982.

——. *The Writing of the Disaster*. Trans. Ann Smock. Lincoln, Nebr.: University of Nebraska Press, 1986.

Booth, Wayne. *The Company We Keep: An Ethics of Fiction*. Berkeley, Calif.: University of California Press, 1988.

Borges, Jorge Luis. *Labyrinths: Selected Stories and Other Writings*. Ed. Donald A. Yates and James E. Irby. New York: New Directions, 1964.

Bourdieu, Pierre. *Distinction: A Social Critique of the Judgement of Taste*. Trans. Richard Nice. Cambridge, Mass.: Harvard University Press, 1984.

——. *The Rules of Art: Genesis and Structure of the Literary Field*. Trans. Susan Emanuel. Stanford, Calif.: Stanford University Press, 1996.

Burke, Kenneth. "Literature as Equipment for Living." *The Philosophy of Literary Form*. 3rd revised edn. Berkeley, Calif.: University of California Press, 1973, pp. 293–304.

Carroll, David. *Paraesthetics: Foucault, Lyotard, Derrida*. New York: Methuen, 1987.

Clark, Timothy. *Derrida, Heidegger, Blanchot: Sources of Derrida's Notion and Practice of Literature*. Cambridge: Cambridge University Press, 1992.

——. *The Theory of Inspiration: Composition as a Crisis of Subjectivity in Romantic and Post-Romantic Writing*. Manchester: Manchester University Press, 1997.

Coetzee, J. M. *Age of Iron*. London: Secker & Warburg, 1990.

——. *Boyhood: Scenes from Provincial Life*. London: Secker & Warburg, 1997.

——. "Confession and Double Thoughts: Tolstoy, Rousseau, Dostoevsky." *Doubling the Point*, pp. 251–93.

——. *Disgrace*. London: Secker & Warburg, 1999.

——. *Doubling the Point: Essays and Interviews*. Ed. David Attwell. Cambridge, Mass.: Harvard University Press, 1992.

——. *Dusklands*. London: Secker & Warburg, 1982.

——. *Elizabeth Costello: Eight Lessons*. London: Secker & Warburg, 2003.

——. *Foe*. London: Secker & Warburg, 1986.

——. *In the Heart of the Country*. London: Secker & Warburg, 1977.

——. *Life & Times of Michael K*. London: Secker & Warburg, 1983.

——. *The Master of Petersburg*. London: Secker & Warburg, 1994.

——. "The Novel Today." *Upstream* 6.1 (1988): 2–5.

——. *Stranger Shores: Essays 1986–1999*. London: Secker & Warburg, 2001.

——. *Waiting for the Barbarians*. London: Secker & Warburg, 1980.

——. "What Is a Classic?" *Stranger Shores*, pp. 1–19.

——. *Youth*. London: Secker & Warburg, 2002.

Cook, Guy. *Discourse and Literature*. Oxford: Oxford University Press, 1994.

Crowther, Paul. *Art and Embodiment: From Aesthetics to Self-Consciousness*. Oxford: Oxford University Press, 1993.

Culler, Jonathan. *On Deconstruction*. London: Routledge & Kegan Paul, 1983.

de Bolla, Peter. *Art Matters*. Cambridge, Mass.: Harvard University Press, 2001.

de Man, Paul. *The Resistance to Theory*. Minneapolis, Minn.: University of Minnesota Press, 1986.

Danto, Arthur C. *The Transfiguration of the Commonplace*. Cambridge, Mass.: Harvard University Press, 1981.

Derrida, Jacques. *Acts of Literature*. Ed. Derek Attridge. New York: Routledge, 1992.

——. *Adieu: to Emmanuel Levinas*. Trans. Pascale-Anne Brault and Michael Naas. Stanford, Calif.: Stanford University Press, 1999.

——. "Afterword: Toward an Ethic of Discussion." *Limited Inc*. Ed. Gerald Graff. Evanston, Ill.: Northwestern University Press, 1988, pp. 111–60.

——. *Aporias: Dying—Awaiting (One Another at) the "Limits of Truth."* Trans. Thomas Dutoit. Stanford, Calif.: Stanford University Press, 1993.

——. "Che cos'è la poesia?" *Points . . . : Interviews 1974–1994.* Ed. Elisabeth Weber. Stanford, Calif.: Stanford University Press, 1992, pp. 288–99.

——. "'Entre le corps écrivant et l'écriture . . .'" (Interview with Daniel Ferrer). *Genesis* 17 (2001): 59–72.

——. "Force of Law: The 'Mystical Foundation of Authority.'" *Deconstruction and the Possibility of Justice.* Ed. Drucilla Cornell, Michel Rosenfeld, and David Gray Carlson. New York: Routledge, 1992, pp. 3–67.

——. *The Gift of Death.* Trans. David Wills. Chicago, Ill.: University of Chicago Press, 1995.

——. "Hostipitality." *Acts of Religion.* Ed. Gil Anidjar. New York: Routledge, 2002, pp. 356–420.

——. "La littérature au secret: Une filiation impossible." *Donner la mort.* Paris: Galilée, 1999, pp. 163–209.

——. "Passions: 'An Oblique Offering.'" *Derrida: A Critical Reader.* Ed. David Wood. Oxford: Blackwell, 1992, pp. 5–35.

——. "Psyche: Invention of the Other." *Acts of Literature*, pp. 311–43.

——. "'A Self-Unsealing Poetic Text': Poetics and Politics of Witnessing." *Revenge of the Aesthetic: The Place of Literature in Theory Today.* Ed. Michael P. Clark. Berkeley, Calif.: University of California Press, 2000, pp. 180–207.

——. "Signature Event Context." *Margins of Philosophy.* Trans. Alan Bass. Chicago, Ill.: University of Chicago Press, 1982, pp. 307–30.

——. "Signsponge." *Acts of Literature*, pp. 344–69.

——. *Specters of Marx: The State of the Debt, the Work of Mourning, and the New International.* Trans. Peggy Kamuf. New York: Routledge, 1994.

——. "'This Strange Institution Called Literature': An Interview with Jacques Derrida." *Acts of Literature*, pp. 33–75.

——. "The University without Condition." *Without Alibi.* Ed. and trans. Peggy Kamuf. Stanford, Calif.: Stanford University Press, 2002, pp. 202–37.

——. "Violence and Metaphysics: An Essay on the Thought of Emmanuel Levinas." *Writing and Difference.* Trans. Alan Bass. Chicago, Ill.: University of Chicago Press, 1978, pp. 79–153.

Derrida, Jacques, and Geoffrey Bennington. *Jacques Derrida.* Trans. Geoffrey Bennington. Chicago, Ill.: University of Chicago Press, 1993.

Derrida, Jacques, and Anne Dufourmantelle. *Of Hospitality.* Trans. Rachel Bowlby. Stanford, Calif.: Stanford University Press, 2000.

Derrida, Jacques, and Pierre-Jean Labarrière. *Altérités.* Paris: Osiris, 1986.

Eagleton, Terry. *The Ideology of the Aesthetic.* Oxford: Blackwell, 1990.

Elam, Diane. *Feminism and Deconstruction: Ms. en Abyme.* London: Routledge, 1994.

Eliot, T. S. "Milton I." *Selected Prose.* Ed. John Hayward. Harmondsworth: Penguin, 1953, pp. 116–24.

——. "Tradition and the Individual Talent." *Selected Essays: New Edition.* New York: Harcourt Brace Jovanovich, 1950, pp. 3–11.

Ellmann, Maud. "Polytropic Man: Paternity, Identity, and Naming in *The Odyssey* and *A Portrait of the Artist as a Young Man.*" *James Joyce: New Perspectives.* Ed. Colin MacCabe. Brighton: Harvester, 1991, pp. 73–104.

Eskin, Michael. *Ethics and Dialogue in the Works of Levinas, Bakhtin, Mandel'shtam, and Celan.* Oxford: Oxford University Press, 2000.

Fish, Stanley E. "Literature in the Reader: Affective Stylistics." *Self-Consuming Artifacts: The Experience of Seventeenth-Century Literature.* Berkeley, Calif.: University of California Press, 1972, pp. 383–427.

Ford, Andrew. *The Origins of Criticism: Literary Culture and Poetic Theory in Classical Greece.* Princeton, N.J.: Princeton University Press, 2002.

Foucault, Michel. *The Archaeology of Knowledge.* Trans. A. M. Sheridan Smith. London: Tavistock, 1972.

——. "Polemics, Politics, and Problematizations: An Interview with Michel Foucault." *Ethics: Subjectivity and Truth.* Ed. Paul Rabinow. New York: New Press, 1997, pp. 111–19.

Furrow, Dwight. *Against Theory: Continental and Analytic Challenges in Moral Philosophy.* New York: Routledge, 1995.

Gadamer, Hans-Georg. "The Relevance of the Beautiful." *"The Relevance of the Beautiful" and Other Essays.* Ed. Robert Bernasconi. Trans. Nicholas Walker. Cambridge: Cambridge University Press, 1986, pp. 3–53.

——. *Truth and Method.* Trans. Joel Weinsheimer and Donald G. Marshall. New York: Crossroad, 1991.

Gammon, Martin. "'Exemplary Originality': Kant on Genius and Imitation." *Journal of the History of Philosophy* 35 (1997): 563–92.

Gasché, Rodolphe. *Inventions of Difference: On Jacques Derrida.* Cambridge, Mass.: Harvard University Press, 1994.

Gaut, Berys, and Dominic McIver Lopes, eds. *The Routledge Companion to Aesthetics.* London: Routledge, 2001.

Glickman, Jack. "Creativity in the Arts." *Philosophy Looks at the Arts: Contemporary Readings in Aesthetics.* Ed. Joseph Margolis. 3rd edn. Philadelphia, Pa.: Temple University Press, 1987, pp. 145–61.

Gombrich, E. H. *Art and Illusion: A Study in the Psychology of Pictorial Representation.* London: Phaidon, 1960.

Hallward, Peter. *Absolutely Postcolonial: Writing between the Singular and the Specific.* Manchester: Manchester University Press, 2001.

Harpham, Geoffrey Galt. *Getting It Right: Language, Literature, and Ethics.* Chicago, Ill.: University of Chicago Press, 1992.

Heidegger, Martin. "The Origin of the Work of Art." *Poetry, Language,*

Thought. Trans. Albert Hofstadter. New York: Harper & Row, 1971, pp. 15–87.

Hobson, Marian. *Jacques Derrida: Opening Lines.* London: Routledge, 1998.

Iser, Wolfgang. *The Act of Reading: A Theory of Aesthetic Response.* Baltimore, Md.: Johns Hopkins University Press, 1978.

——. *The Implied Reader: Patterns of Communication in Prose Fiction from Bunyan to Beckett.* Baltimore, Md.: Johns Hopkins University Press, 1974.

Jameson, Fredric. *The Political Unconscious: Narrative as a Socially Symbolic Act.* Ithaca, N.Y.: Cornell University Press, 1981.

Jauss, Hans Robert. *Toward an Ethic of Reception.* Trans. Timothy Bahti. Minneapolis, Minn.: University of Minnesota Press, 1982.

Johnson, Barbara. *The Critical Difference: Essays in the Contemporary Rhetoric of Reading.* Baltimore, Md.: Johns Hopkins University Press, 1980.

Joyce, James. *Ulysses.* Ed. Hans Walter Gabler with Wolfhard Steppe and Claus Melchior. 3 vols. New York: Garland, 1984.

Kamuf, Peggy, ed. *A Derrida Reader: Between the Blinds.* New York: Columbia University Press, 1991.

Kant, Immanuel. *Critique of Judgment.* Trans. Werner S. Pluhar. Indianapolis, Ind.: Hackett Publishing Company, 1987.

Keenan, Thomas. *Fables of Responsibility: Aberrations and Predicaments in Ethics and Politics.* Stanford, Calif.: Stanford University Press, 1997.

Kivy, Peter. *The Possessor and the Possessed: Handel, Mozart, Beethoven, and the Idea of Musical Genius.* New Haven, Conn.: Yale University Press, 2001.

Kuhn, Thomas S. *The Structure of Scientific Revolutions.* 2nd edn. Chicago, Ill.: University of Chicago Press, 1970.

Lahr, John. "Making It Real: How Mike Nichols Re-created Comedy and Himself." *New Yorker* (February 21 and 28, 2000): 196–214.

Leavis, F. R. *Revaluation: Tradition and Development in English Poetry.* Harmondsworth: Penguin, 1964.

Lecercle, Jean-Jacques. "Cantor, Lacan, Mao, Beckett, *même combat*: The Philosophy of Alain Badiou." *Radical Philosophy* 93 (January–February 1999): 6–13.

——. *Interpretation as Pragmatics.* London: Macmillan, 1999.

——. *The Philosophy of Nonsense: The Intuitions of Victorian Nonsense Literature.* London: Routledge, 1994.

——. *Philosophy through the Looking-Glass: Language, Nonsense, Desire.* London: Hutchinson, 1985.

——. *The Violence of Language.* London: Routledge, 1990.

Lentricchia, Frank, and Andrew Dubois, eds. *Close Reading: The Reader.* Durham, N.C.: Duke University Press, 2003.

Levinas, Emmanuel. *Otherwise than Being, or Beyond Essence.* Trans. Alphonso Lingis. Pittsburgh, Pa.: Duquesne University Press, 1981.

——. "Paul Celan: From Being to the Other." *Proper Names.* Trans. Michael B. Smith. Stanford, Calif.: Stanford University Press, 1996, pp. 40–6.

——. "Reality and Its Shadow." *The Levinas Reader.* Ed. Sean Hand. Oxford: Blackwell, 1989, pp. 129–43.

——. *Totality and Infinity: An Essay on Exteriority.* Trans. Alphonso Lingis. Pittsburgh, Pa.: Duquesne University Press, 1969.

Levinson, Jerrold. *The Oxford Handbook of Aesthetics.* Oxford: Oxford University Press, 2003.

Lyotard, Jean-François. *The Differend: Phrases in Dispute.* Trans. Georges Van Den Abbeele. Minneapolis, Minn.: University of Minnesota Press, 1988.

——. *The Postmodern Condition: A Report on Knowledge.* Trans. Geoff Bennington and Brian Massumi. Minneapolis, Minn.: University of Minnesota Press, 1984.

——. *The Postmodern Explained.* Ed. Julian Pefanis and Morgan Thomas. Minneapolis, Minn.: University of Minnesota Press, 1993.

Lyotard, Jean-François, and Jean-Loup Thébaud. *Just Gaming.* Trans. Wlad Godzich. Minneapolis, Minn.: University of Minnesota Press, 1985.

Macherey, Pierre. *A Theory of Literary Production.* Trans. Geoffrey Wall. London: Routledge & Kegan Paul, 1978.

McKeon, Michael. *The Origins of the English Novel, 1600–1740.* Baltimore, Md.: Johns Hopkins University Press, 1987.

Maley, Willy. "Spectres of Engels." *Ghosts: Deconstruction, Psychoanalysis, History.* Ed. Peter Buse and Andrew Stott. London: Macmillan, 1999, pp. 23–49.

Miller, J. Hillis. *The Ethics of Reading: Kant, de Man, Eliot, Trollope, James, and Benjamin.* New York: Columbia University Press, 1987.

Nussbaum, Martha C. *Love's Knowledge: Essays on Philosophy and Literature.* New York: Oxford University Press, 1990.

Parker, Andrew, and Eve Kosofsky Sedgwick, eds. *Performativity and Performance.* New York: Routledge, 1995.

Pound, Ezra. *ABC of Reading.* London: Faber & Faber, 1951.

Rabaté, Jean-Michel. *Joyce upon the Void: The Genesis of Doubt.* New York: St Martin's, 1991.

Rampley, Matthew. "Creativity." *British Journal of Aesthetics* 38 (1998): 265–78.

Rand, Richard. "Ozone: An Essay on Keats." *Post-structuralist Readings of English Poetry.* Ed. Richard Machin and Christopher Norris. Cambridge: Cambridge University Press, 1987, pp. 294–307.

Readings, Bill. *Introducing Lyotard: Art and Politics.* London: Routledge, 1991.

Richards, I. A. *Practical Criticism.* London: Routledge & Kegan Paul, 1929.

——. *Principles of Literary Criticism.* 2nd edn. London: Routledge & Kegan Paul, 1926.

Robbins, Bruce. *Secular Vocations: Intellectuals, Professionalism, Culture.* London: Verso, 1993.

Robbins, Jill. *Altered Reading: Levinas and Literature.* Chicago, Ill.: University of Chicago Press, 1999.

Rosen, Charles. *The Classical Style: Haydn, Mozart, Beethoven.* London: Faber & Faber, 1971.

——. *Schoenberg.* Glasgow: Fontana/Collins, 1976.

Rosenblatt, Louise M. *The Reader, the Text, the Poem: The Transactional Theory of the Literary Work.* Carbondale, Ill.: Southern Illinois University Press, 1978.

Royle, Nicholas. *After Derrida.* Manchester: Manchester University Press, 1995.

Royston, Robert, ed. *Black Poets in South Africa.* London: Heinemann, 1973.

Russell, D. A., and M. Winterbottom, eds. *Ancient Literary Criticism.* Oxford: Oxford University Press, 1972.

Said, Edward W. *Musical Elaborations.* London: Chatto & Windus, 1991.

Sartre, Jean-Paul. *What is Literature?* Trans. Bernard Frechtman. London: Methuen, 1950.

Saussure, Ferdinand de. *Course in General Linguistics.* Trans. Wade Baskin. Glasgow: Fontana/Collins, 1974.

Scarry, Elaine. *On Beauty and Being Just.* Princeton, N.J.: Princeton University Press, 1999.

Sher, Antony. *Beside Myself: An Autobiography.* London: Hutchinson, 2001.

Spivak, Gayatri Chakravorty. Translator's Preface to Jacques Derrida, *Of Grammatology.* Baltimore, Md.: Johns Hopkins University Press, 1976.

Staten, Henry. *Wittgenstein and Derrida.* Lincoln, Nebr.: University of Nebraska Press, 1984.

Steiner, George. *Grammars of Creation.* London: Faber & Faber, 2001.

Trilling, Lionel. "The Sense of the Past." *The Liberal Imagination: Essays on Literature and Society.* London: Mercury Books, 1961, pp. 181–97.

Vendler, Helen. *The Music of What Happens: Poems, Poets, Critics.* Cambridge, Mass.: Harvard University Press, 1988.

Weber, Samuel. "Ambivalence: The Humanities and the Study of Literature." *Institution and Interpretation.* Minneapolis, Minn.: University of Minnesota Press, 1987, pp. 132–52.

Weitz, Morris. "The Role of Theory in Aesthetics." *Philosophy Looks at the Arts: Contemporary Readings in Aesthetics.* Ed. Joseph Margolis. 3rd edn. Philadelphia, Pa.: Temple University Press, 1987, pp. 143–53.

Wiener, Norbert. *Invention: the Care and Feeding of Ideas.* Cambridge, Mass.: M.I.T. Press, 1993.

Williams, Raymond. *Keywords: A Vocabulary of Culture and Society.* Rev. edn. New York: Oxford University Press, 1983.

——. *Marxism and Literature*. Oxford: Oxford University Press, 1977.

Wills, David. "Derrida and Aesthetics: Lemming (Reframing the Abyss)." *Derrida and the Humanities*. Ed. Tom Cohen. Cambridge: Cambridge University Press, 2001, pp. 108–31.

Wittgenstein, Ludwig. *Philosophical Investigations*. Trans. G. E. M. Anscombe. 3rd edn. Oxford: Blackwell, 1968.

Young, Edward. *Conjectures on Original Composition*. Leeds: The Scolar Press, 1966 [1759].

Young, Robert, ed. *Untying the Text: A Post-Structuralist Reader*. London: Routledge & Kegan Paul, 1981.

Ziarek, Krzysztof. *The Force of Art*. Stanford, Calif.: Stanford University Press, 2004.

Index

Adorno, Theodor W. 6, 7, 14, 114, 142
advertisements 85–6
Aeschylus 47, 121
aesthetics 3, 11–13, 93, 136; *see also* beauty
allegory 96
Altdorfer, Albrecht 38
alterity (otherness) 2, 15, 30, 120, 136–7; and Blake's "The Sick Rose" 67, 69; creation and 19–21, 24, 26, 79; creative reading and 79, 80, 81, 83; cultural distance and 52; demands of 131; ethics and 126–8; as event 127; familiarity and 76, 138; form and 107, 108, 110, 114, 115; generality of term 29; idioculture and 22; and the influence of Levinas 141; introduction of 121; and invention/inventiveness 42–3, 44, 46, 48, 53, 136; literary events and 59; moment of registering 27; natural objects and 102; and the performance of a work 87, 98; pleasurable apprehension of 76–7; and the possible risk to a culture 60; and responsibility for the other 120,
124, 125; responsiveness to 91, 129, 130; and singularity 29, 33, 63, 67; translation of works and 74; uniqueness and 64; welcoming 60, 83, 115, 137; Western philosophy and 84; *see also* the other
Anderson, Benedict 86
Aristotle 49, 75, 84, 97, 107
Attwell, David 140
Austen, Jane 20, 35
authoredness 101–3, 110–11, 136

Bach, J. S. 39, 55
Badiou, Alain 142
Bakhtin, Mikhail 141, 143
Barthes, Roland 103, 143
beauty 11, 12, 14, 97; *see also* aesthetics
Beethoven, Ludwig van 40
Benjamin, Walter 59, 64
Bennett, Tony 143
Bennington, Geoffrey 142
Bernasconi, Robert 141
Bernstein, J. M. 142
Blake, William 19, 65–70, 71–2
Blanchot, Maurice 7, 142
Bolden, Buddy 38
Booth, Wayne 76
Borges, Jorge Luis 65

performance 2, 6, 87, 95–106, 136;
and form 108, 111, 115, 118;
and meaning 109; pleasure in 119
Petrarch 75
philosophy 49, 56, 84, 86, 143
phonemes 57, 58
Picasso, Pablo 48
Plato 12, 107, 121
pleasure 76, 78, 119, 131
poetry: application of term 61;
Aristotle on 75; and the couplet
39; distinctiveness of 71–2;
Donne 44, 46, 47; form and 108,
111–18; and iambic pentameter
50; inventiveness and 45; metrical
arrangements of 31; performance
of 97, 98–100; and poulter's
measure 50; privileged over prose
120; and singularity 65–70;
temporality of 104; translations of
73–4
politics: and artistic practices 38;
instrumentalism and 7, 8, 9, 13,
119–20; see also ideology
Pope, Alexander 77
popular culture 61
postcolonial studies 32
poulter's measure 50, 82
Pound, Ezra 37, 91
Pre-Raphaelites 37, 49
production (vs. creation) 25
prose 72, 120; see also novels
psychoanalysis 26
psychology 18, 85
purposiveness 57, 100–1

Rabelais, François 46–7
race 30
racism 31, 113, 116, 117–18
Rawls, John 86
re-reading 88–9, 93
reading: act-event of 59, 105;
conventions of 119; creative

79–83, 85, 86, 88; ethics of 130;
instrumental approach to 8, 9; as
invention 92–3; Iser's theory of
144; literary 86–7, 130; and the
literary event 59; performative
109; re-reading 88–9, 93; and the
real-time nature of poetry 71–2;
as response 89–92; temporality
and 104–5; transactional 144;
verbal invention and 56
Readings, Bill 142
realist fiction 97
'reality effect' 7–8
reception: cultural conventions and
49; of inventions 43–4; primary
modes of 56
referentiality 95–6, 109, 118, 119
response and responsiveness 89–92,
93, 118, 133, 137; ethical
response 128–31; everyday life
and 135; and the performance of
a work 98; and responsibility for
the other 120, 123, 124, 125–6,
128; to the singular otherness of
a person 33, 34
responsibility: ethical implications of
126–8; for the other 120, 123–8,
135, 137
rhyme 66, 68, 69
rhythm 66, 67–8, 69, 71–2, 76, 99
Richards, I. A. 90, 131
Richardson, Samuel 45
risk: and creativity 124; in the
process of creation 26; and
responsibility for the other 124,
126; of welcoming the other 60
Robbins, Jill 141
Rosa, Salvator 47
Rosenblatt, Louise M. 144
Russian Formalism 39, 143

Said, Edward 105
Sartre, Jean-Paul 143